ARCHITECTURE DESIGN INNOVATION PROGRAM

INTERROGATING POP IN ARCHITECTURE

Editor Daniela Konrad
Collaborating Editor Jason Danziger

ARCHITECTURE DESIGN INNOVATION PROGRAM

INTERROGATING POP IN ARCHITECTURE

Editor Daniela Konrad
Collaborating Editor Jason Danziger

With a preface by Jürgen Mayer H.

Editor. Daniela Konrad

Collaborating Editor. Jason Danziger

Publication Team. Christoph Bukowski,
Samsarah Lilja, Sybille Paulsen, Lisa Plücker

Exclusive Distributor
Ernst Wasmuth Verlag Tübingen · Berlin
www.wasmuth-verlag.de

Printed in Germany
ISBN 978-3-8030-0694-3
July, 2008

ARCHITECTURE DESIGN INNOVATION PROGRAM
FG ENTWERFEN UND INNENRAUMPLANUNG
TECHNISCHE UNIVERSITÄT BERLIN, GERMANY

CONTENTS

PREFACE

Jürgen Mayer H.

Over the last few decades, architecture has shifted as it reacts to the fundamental changes our society has experienced due to the introduction of new technologies and modes of expression. Like everything else, this phenomenal shift has been increasing in speed over the last few years, and architecture has recently become a profession oscillating between technological design and sculptural expression, often taking new positions which might transcend traditional tasks and design methods. In other words, architects have begun to allow their practice to be influenced and affected by a series of phenomena that, earlier, didn't seem to play an important role in their profession.

While architects have always tried to provoke changes through a distinguished positioning within the architectural and building discourse, recently some architects have been further challenging conventions by offering visionary designs which offer the possibility of truly re-defining our built environment. These designs seek to address the obvious need for structurally, technologically and/or ecologically innovative designs, but also strive to offer spatially and visually attractive arrangements which might seem surprising but can be understood by the masses. As a result, many homogeneous urban fabrics have been punctuated with landmark-like sculptures and stand-alone objects. Thus, architecture has become a culturally legible attractor for many, often using new technologies to enable the erection of fascinating and unexpected buildings.

For this reason, to investigate and interrogate the cultural phenomenon of POP in architecture means to directly explore the crucial and essential criteria of our contemporary building practice. Unlike Postmodernism, New Urbanism, or Critical Reconstruction, which all operate through mechanisms of seduction centered around the creation of a consensual understanding of the past, POP culture always refers to the means of today and the understanding of the many, and as such can be described as the contemporaneous expression of any given social context. As POP art in the 1960s began to open up a new market for artists and swamp the masses with eye-catching art, architecture has begun working increasingly with this same methodology today.

The media is never far behind such shifts, and thus there is a growing tendency for more and more of these buildings to become widely publicized, attracting the public's attention to the discipline in a manner previously unknown. Furthermore, augmenting ambitions amongst architects has driven them to suggest ever more solutions and places for multi-purpose uses and temporary structures. Again, this closely follows the basic axiom of POP culture that people always find a way to express themselves in their given context. Thus, this investigation of POP phenomena in architecture should be understood as an invitation to explore a new reading of our contemporary architectural discourse and building practice.

INTERROGATING POP IN ARCHITECTURE
Notes on Our Intention and Teaching Method

This book seeks to provoke, push, and contribute to the current discourse on a series of aspects of POP in architecture. Its positions have grown out of process-based research undertaken at the Technische Universität Berlin together with a motley crew of invited international and interdisciplinary guests and graduate students alike ... During the winter semester of 2006/7 we experimented with an interrogative teaching method, designed to optimize group interaction and collaborative research responsibility within our design studio. Thus, the project was seen as a collective inquiry, looking to understand the cultural phenomenon known as POP and focused on the central question of clarifying its uneasy relationship to architecture. Our plan was to establish a working definition of the term POP, and then, to explore a range of POP architecture with an eye towards making a design proposal. Among other questions, we wanted to know: How can POP be translated into architecture from other areas of POP culture? How has the wider public adapted to an age of abstracted POP images selling brands instead of pure imagery? How has the pure medial power of the image influenced architecture in recent years? And why and how is the presence of POP culture and POP architecture an initiator for a new positioning of architecture in today's society?

Experiment: Structure and process

The experiment's high point was a two-day symposium in which students and guest critics alike established positions concerning POP. All participants of the seminar, as well as two advanced students working on their diploma, were seeking to push the group into a deep inquiry of the particularities of POP in architecture. Students, guest critics, studio leaders, all shared in responsibility to push the research ever further. For this reason, we constructed a project curriculum designed to provide rhythm to the project and ensure that students were making progress on the larger design issues of the studio. It was composed of five major elements:

1// Design exercises and creative workshops
2// Field trips
3// Project design (i.e., Architectural responses to the subject of research)
4// Preparation for and participation in our group symposium
5// A project archive (leading to the book you are holding in your hands)

For each exercise students were required to produce a response to a particular design question or issue, whose answer would then become an element of the final project. The exercises also required students to work with a range of design tools, often shifting between them in order to encourage the students to build an active design research practice. Thus, students began by researching and expressing the term POP in collages, which, over time, mutated into site-reaction sketches, then becoming models at various scales, and further, into drawings, and further models. Critical during these phases was the constant shift of tools, questioning solutions and thereby strengthening and pushing our inquiry onwards. Workshops and field trips enriched the rhythm of the studio.

These gave our group a series of mid- and long-term goals around which to note the progress of our search. Notable in this series was a workshop on "branding" which encouraged the group to develop their program for the site, and one on "semiotics" which led to an in-depth investigation of the role of the image in architecture. A visit to Zaha Hadid's Phaeno Center in Wolfsburg, another to OMA's Dutch Embassy in Berlin and the Hans Otto Theatre by Gottfried Böhm in Potsdam widened our horizon on contemporary building designs. And a visit to our site, the area of the former Nordbahnhof in Berlin Mitte, finally allowed the students to implement their first ideas on POP in architecture on a "real" site.

Forum

We also created an ongoing, living forum in which to encourage the students to push their research further than that done in a normal studio. This found different forms during the project. It could be described as a type of integrated independent study, in which students could "extend" or "deepen" the project as per their inspiration. These project extensions were available in two directions, either in terms of "theory" – researching a figure or event integral to the POP story, or via the definition of a POP "phenomenon" – in which students would select critical urban or architectural spaces from the project which they would then further elaborate. During a series of public presentations, TU Berlin internal and external guest critics discussed the works in progress, giving life to our forum. These alternative points of view were invaluable to us as a group as they showed us where the projects needed to be strengthened and continued. As mentioned above, the highlight of the studio and the culmination of the larger group's efforts was a two day, intensive symposium titled "ARCHITECTURE reTURNS to POP." Pushing beyond the standard final jury model, we instead invited five international, interdisciplinary guests to work with us for a day of intensive group inquiry. The concept of the event was to create a horizontal platform to enable the exchange and contrast of positions on architecture and POP. Thus, the symposium was formed around blocks, each grounded in the position of one of our external critics. Throughout two very intense days of group discussion, critique, and lecturing a series of positions on POP in architecture have been raised and discussed. These blocks of inquiry then formed the seeds for the chapter structure of this book, which should be understood as both an archive and an extension of our forum process.

Invitation

The book you now hold in your hands represents the distilled efforts of nearly fifty persons, working together in order to understand and react in a myriad of ways to the strange and vibrant cultural phenomenon which is POP, and to find a way to extract the POP from architecture. We hope you enjoy it.

Daniela Konrad + Jason Danziger
Berlin, 2008

0 INTRODUCTION

POP PHENOMENA IN ARCHITECTURE

Daniela Konrad

POP PHENOMENA IN ARCHITECTURE

Daniela Konrad

Only the realization of utopias will make man happy and release him from his frustrations!
[Wolf Vostell]

So gesehen handelt es sich beim Populären um eine besonders voraussetzungsarme, zugängliche und deshalb demokratische Form von Ästhetik, von kulturellen Gegenständen und Ereignissen. POP ist eine dem Kapitalismus zeitgenössischen Stadiums entsprechende Art der Fiktionalisierung, des Seelenbalsams, der Massenrituale: die "Popmoderne."
[Jochen Bonz]

On POP culture

POP refers to popular culture. This cultural phenomenon is linked to widespread aspects and attributes of the general public that appear out of a vernacular society over time. POP has mostly been associated with music and art, but it is finding relevance in the world of architecture and urban theory, now more than ever. A new trend is arising – many of today's architects aspire to or are becoming "POP stars." They design buildings which are frequented by a broad spectrum of the public and they present illustrations of their built and unbuilt architectural proposals in the communication media. There, we become aware of buildings and whole urban conglomerations operating as backdrops, setting the stage for products or serving directly as icons for individual institutions or even whole cities.

POP culture is mass culture, an easily understandable and accessible culture, appreciated by a large public audience, affordable, and maybe even cheap. Furthermore, POP culture has the potential to reflect and exaggerate, or to radically oppose a predominant condition. Due to these characteristics, POP culture has often been a stimulus for ground-breaking ideas and fundamental changes. Participation in POP culture and the consumption of its products seem to even stimulate a behavioral reaction from people. Large groups of people go to the same event, or buy the same objects. Thus POP culture may link and subsequently replace elite and subcultures, merging people from high society to low-income groups to form one powerful community.

Both the establishment of a society of consumption and consumer capitalism, and the ongoing globalization of economies and communication, have enabled the acceptance, success, and expansion of POP. Interestingly, John Fiske, a British sociologist and researcher of cultural studies, claims that increasing consumption and participation in POP culture leads to cultural differentiation and identity. In fact, while the term "POP" seems to be obsessively used and linked to a superficial mass attraction, it is important to understand that POP culture is always arising out of reactions to a dominant cultural phenomenon. These reactions may be subversive and undermining, or adaptive, as they accept or even strengthen a specific contemporary condition. POP is not solely a mass-cultural trend but a cultural expression and statement. Furthermore, POP phenomena are not static and clearly defined cultural movements. Rather, POP culture is reinventing itself constantly, as society is evolving and changing. This means that once everybody has a desirable POP object, it loses its seductive character and people start to lose interest. This process continues until the POP cycle has reached the point where even the masses are not interested in the POP object anymore and it disappears; then, due to another social or cultural reason, a new POP object arises.

Borrowing an iconography from daily life of mass culture, one of the constant characteristics of POP culture is the fact that it claims a triumphal return of the object and the image. And yet another aspect is its economical factor. Goods classified as POP are affordable and therefore easy to obtain and possess. And they are, or need to be, mass-produced.

Indeed, it seems inevitable that the everyday culture that affected art needed to, at one point, affect architecture as well.

To discuss POP phenomena in architecture the traditional characteristics of POP culture defined here are important, but also other aspects of contemporary architecture need to be considered. Because even though POP architecture doesn't seem to be a topical and appreciated term in architectural discourse, POP culture cannot be treated as an anachronism; it is a phenomenon that definitely has affected and promoted architectural tendencies in the 20th century, and it is increasingly influencing today's building practice. But which aspects have led to modern POP phenomena in architecture, and in what way were and are they expressed?

POP in Architecture – a historical overview

There have been numerous discussions and investigations on the existence, occurrence, or expressions of POP culture in architecture. To be able to gain a deeper insight in the term "POP architecture," a condensed historical overview of architects working with POP culture or critics discussing the appearance of POP phenomena in architecture introduces a series of important aspects in this field.

POP culture slowly started to penetrate into our Western society with the period of industrialization. The structural societal changes taking place at that time gave people of the working classes the opportunity to participate in the creation of cultural statements. While high-culture and low-culture opposed each other for decades, it was at the beginning of the 20th century that this dichotomy began to disappear. The criticism of existing political and social conditions resulted in a series of radical ideas. Especially in the fields of music, art, and literature, these changes were rapidly manifested.

Just what is it that makes today's homes so different, so appealing?
Artist: Richard Hamilton

Yet with POP art emerging in the 1950s, an important step towards a global appearance of POP culture was made. The provenance of the phenomenon of POP architecture therefore needs to be linked with the origins of POP art in Great Britain. In the 1950s, a group of artists, architects and critics surrounding Eduardo Paolozzi and Richard Hamilton founded the Independent Group in London. In collaboration with his group members, Richard Hamilton created the collage *Just what is it that makes today's homes so different, so appealing?* This photomontage refers to a society of consumerism, showing an overflow of modern and commonly known consumer goods appreciated by two almost naked figures. Being part of the everyday life of many, the items depicted carry the illusory idea of familiarity, or even intimacy, and suggest a straightforward approachability of art.

> *Gropius wrote a book on grain silos,*
> *Le Corbusier one on aeroplanes,*
> *and Charlotte Perriand brought a new*
> *object to the office every morning;*
> *but today we collect ads.*
> [The Smithsons]

The architects Alison and Peter Smithson and the cultural and architectural critic Reyner Banham were part of the Independent Group and played an important part in the fledgling British POP art movement. The Smithsons were the architectural minds of the team, but it was the artist Richard Hamilton who specified the POP spirit in a letter to the Smithsons, calling it "popular, transient, expendable, low cost, mass-produced, young, witty, sexy, gimmicky, glamorous, big business." While the POP movement started to spread rapidly and allowed a wide range of expression within the artists' world, architecture was still dominated by the Modern Movement. Slowly, it began to define a new approach, which in the '50s and '60s led to an architecture that can be described as POP. Next to their engagement in the Independent Group, the Smithsons were part of the leaders of the British School of New Brutalism and associated with Team X, a group of architects assembled in 1953 at the 9th Congress of CIAM. Revolting against philosophies of high Modernism and an austere and traditional society, the Smithsons were uncompromising in their search for a new approach to modernist architecture which – like the pre-war International Style – would exploit the low cost pragmatism of pre-fabricated components and mass-produced materials. They developed a fascination for people's everyday living situations and coined the maxim "as found" in opposition to the aesthetic doctrines of the Modern Movement. The project most clearly expressing their POP ideas was the *House of the Future*, a visionary home designed for the 1956 *Daily Mail Ideal Home Exhibition* in London. The house was composed of a mass-produceable plastic structure full of innovative futuristic features like easy-to-clean corners, and gadgets like a "shower-blow-dryer-sunlamp" inspired by sci-fi movie imagery of the time. Their design can be described as an optimistic art of dwelling. And even though it was alien to their contemporaneous housing designs, the project was an important contribution to their research on new concepts of "place" and "territory." It was supposed to be a desirable and fashionable product for people and a clear statement about the possibility of combining technology-oriented and mass-produceable design with a new glamorous and blissful lifestyle.

its technical performance, the mainstream customer is not knowledgeable enough to buy for technical innovation, only to be attracted to a beautiful object. Meeting the young architects Warren Chalk, Peter Cook, Dennis Crompton, David Greene, Ron Herron and Michael Webb, who formed the group Archigram (from ARCHItecture und teleGRAM), working on technology-fascinated design and an imaged-packed architecture, Banham described them as pioneers of POP architecture. With extravagant-subversive projects like the *Walking City* or the *Plug-in City*, Archigram focused on developing megastructural utopias for the city of the future.

In fact, Archigram not only designed these fantasies but also started to distribute them in the form of the identically named magazine in London. It was a cheap and mass-produced magazine that contained comic-like illustrations, poems, and artistic or architectural collages. While on the one hand the influence of POP art was obvious, on the other hand a manifestation of independent and innovative ideas on contemporary spaces was crucial to the group's work. They wanted to express their opposition to the architectural style of their times and tried to push the idea of reaching the masses with their magazine. Yet these first attempts of POP architecture didn't reach the general public, and remained a small niche within the future development of architecture.

Reyner Banham argued that the future development of the machine age results in a POP age, where form does not only follow function, but also mediates an image.

Reyner Banham pushed the reconditioning of Modernism by pointing out that a machine can directly influence the design of a building, meaning that technological knowledge liberates the designers' mind to use it as the fountainhead for their creative brainchild; and vice versa. In his article *A Throw-away Aesthetic* Banham argues that the convincing look of a product should be a selling point. While the product developer is its overall master and responsible for

Equally fascinated with the ordinary, Cedric Price designed buildings for an emerging leisure society; best-known is the *Fun Palace* in London, developed in collaboration with the theatre director Joan Littlewood. Price suggested a variable high-tech space that was accessible all day, for everybody, able to house diverse unspecified events – an unconventional proposal for a building that enables people to enjoy their own creative lives. Other groups, such as Superstudio or Archizoom, introduced aspects form POP culture in defiance of existing ideologies. Superstudio expressed their disillusionment with modernist architecture in form of photo-collages showing pessimist and absurd visions, as *The Continuous Monument*. Instead, Archizoom proposed ironic-utopian objects, as the *Superonda-sofa*, which invited unconventional postures by its waved shape, to initiate a "Revolution of Kitsch: mass consumption, POP art, and an industrial-commercial language" (Andrea Branzi). At the end of the '60s, Dick Higgins and Wolf Vostell, two artists from Great Britain and Germany, continued this utopian trend and published a book named *Poparchitektur. Concept Art*. While the content of the book appears superficial, their message is clear: They opposed purely economical considerations for architectural propositions and claimed that the way buildings are experienced had widely suffered. If architecture is able to house only people, they stated, it has lost its opportunity to offer excitement, joy, or emotional impressions.

Parallel to these developments, another movement started: the theme park industry. Derived from the tradition of the amusement parks and pleasure gardens (e.g., Coney Island), a new theme park opened in 1955: *Disneyland* in Anaheim, California – and it had a path-breaking and lasting effect on the amusement park industry. Architects were mostly replaced by film directors, who worked on the in-scene-setting of Walt Disney's popular animated characters.

Theme park architecture is rarely designed by architects; it is erected to provide enjoyment and present the elusive idea of perfect worlds, hiding technical mechanisms and infrastructures.

Today there is a wide range of theme parks, offering everything from leisure activities to whole cityscapes with permanent housing. Extreme paradigms of this kind are found in Japan. One example is *The Little World Museum of Man* in Inuyama-City (inaugurated in 1983), where one can see characteristic buildings from most of the different countries in the world in a distance that you can easily walk. Another is the *Huis Ten Bosch* theme park (inaugurated in 1992); it is a recreation of Holland that displays real size copies of old Dutch buildings. These theme parks are highly frequented and count as tourist attractions. Their architecture can be considered POP architecture. But, in contrast to Archigram's or Superstudio's proposals for illusions, theme park architecture has no subversive undertone or feeling and can be rather discussed as populist architecture, fulfilling the desires of the masses. Although buildings in theme parks can be understood as "niche architecture," our environment today is invaded by constructions which are not designed by architects or specialists in general. Thus the current involvement of architects and urbanists in event culture and shopping malls can be discussed as new experiments in this POP domain.

In the 1970s, Robert Venturi, Denise Scott Brown and Steven Izenour began another iteration of the POP architecture idea, one linked to mainstream architecture. Their intention was to call for architects to be more receptive to the tastes and values of common people, and less obsessed with the creation of their own intellectual-artistic monuments. For their research on the semiotics of the American cities, Venturi, Scott Brown and Izenour focused on the city of Las Vegas and the suburban family idylls in Levittown, as a representative for the residential quarters in the United States. With their provocative publication *Learning from Las Vegas: The Forgotten Symbolism of Architectural Form*, they placed a revolutionary case study on the iconography of buildings, making a strong statement towards vernacular architecture and the ordinary structures of everyday life. The publication reinvigorated architectural design with symbolic content, which the team found during their analysis and documentation of the physical form of Las Vegas. To describe the significance of this architectural "mainstream" style, Venturi, Scott Brown and Izenour coined the terms "duck" (a literal translation of the content as a sculptural symbol) and "decorated shed" (the generic box with attached signs and ornaments conveying the function of the building), which were widely discussed in the architectural discourse in the 1970s and extremely influential to the Postmodern movement.

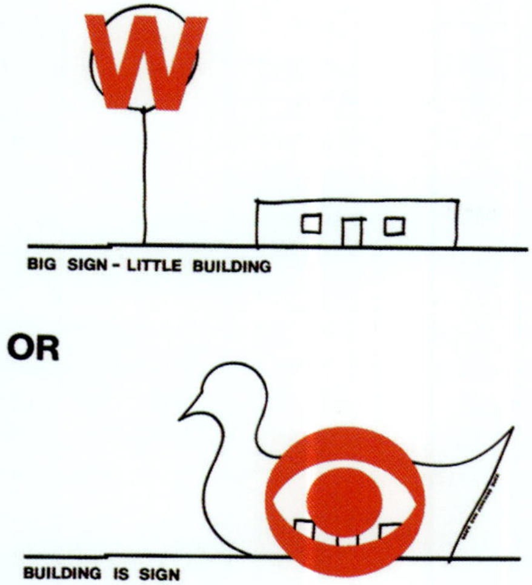

"Duck" and "decorated shed" study
Venturi, Scott Brown and Associates

The almost theatrical staging of architecture as a result of the unlimited media-presence is a phenomenon that the historian Daniel Boorstin had predicted in 1961 in his study *The Image: A Guide to Pseudo-Events in America*, and that Umberto Eco calls "hyperreality." To some extent, one can say that the architecture of Las Vegas can be understood as yet another indicator of today's augmented post-realities and digital designs. Also, Robert Venturi coined the maxim "Less is a bore" as expressionist antidote to Ludwig Mies van der Rohe's famous modernist dictum "Less is more." Finally, the architecture statements of Venturi, Scott Brown and Izenour led the discourse on POP phenomena in architecture towards stagnation, and the studies of the popular aspects of Las Vegas were rapidly opposed by many architects. Even though other architects such as Archigram and Superstudio continued to work with the POP aspects of architecture in the mid and late '70s, POP architecture seemed to disappear slowly but steadily, or at least to be avoided.

Criticism of Modern architecture has been ongoing. In 1981, Tom Wolfe wrote in the introduction to his book *From Bauhaus to our House:* "O beautiful, for spacious skies, for amber waves of grain, has there ever been another place on earth where so many people of wealth and power have paid for and put up with so much architecture they detested as within the blessed borders today? ... Every $900,000 summer house in the north woods of Michigan or on the shore of Long Island has so many pipe railings, ramps, hob-treated metal spiral stairways, sheets of industrial plate glass, banks of tungsten-halogen lamps, and white cylindrical shapes, it looks like an insecticide refinery." While the avant-garde architects were afraid of indulging in populist ideas, the majority of the population felt disregarded by the creators of their homes or public buildings. The gap between the ideas of the masses about how to live and the architects who were designing and constructing their homes increased. But Robert Venturi's and Denise Scott Brown's interventions could not convince the architects that popular ideas could be an indicator of how to design in the future, and the turn towards a more accessible architecture did not yet happen.

Although several modest attempts have been made, the POP movement can be observed to reappear first with Rem Koolhaas in the late '80s and early '90s. Even though Koolhaas, who was trained as a scriptwriter, cannot be understood as a stand-in POP architect, he raised important issues within this context. He does not refer to the bare aesthetics of popular culture, but rather compares and combines the Modern Movement with a POP movement, resulting in designs guided by semiotic formulations of social, cultural, and urban conditions. Even though his projects are based on an extended research and a sophisticated approach, Koolhaas attracted a wider public with his architecture almost from the beginning of his career, with the Kunsthal in Rotterdam, built in 1987. Consequently, Rem Koolhaas has been able to place himself as a trademark within the architectural market.

While Rem Koolhaas has left a vast percentage of architects in a state of paralysis trying to reproduce or at least rethink his oeuvre, the architect Frank Gehry started to establish an architecture of spectacle. His buildings have become tourist attractions, especially the Guggenheim Museum in Bilbao, Spain, which has acquired the image of a generator of growth and prosperity for a whole city. Even if this image might be illusory, an increasing number of clients want to use his services to (re-)establish identity through similarly spectacular and expressionist designs. However, the risk of these productions is the neglect of the inner logic or the program of a building due to iconography alone.

Many contemporary buildings carry the intention of becoming visual signs and icons for a place and strive to attract the masses not only through program but through sensation. Hence, these buildings enable and even provoke a completely different spatial experience for the public.

Gehry's colleague Peter Eisenman describes this enormous public success as "Bilbao Effect," and talks about the astonishing process of architecture dissolving into pure spectacle. But Frank Gehry's popularity represents the taste and opinion of a wider public, and his architecture does respond to the thoughts and dreams of the majority. Though architects often disagree with Gehry's architecture and downsize his famous reputation, it seems that the success he had with the museum in Bilbao cannot be exceeded, but only copied ... Just recently, Zaha Hadid won the competition for the Guggenheim Museum in Vilnius, Lithuania. Her design proposal incorporates the characteristic conceptual elements of her architectural language. A resemblance to her Phaeno Center in Wolfsburg is undeniable and precisely this resemblance is a strength of the design. Hadid has developed a corporate architectural language for her buildings; a language that has become globally known and recognizable. Today, this may be the jury of an architecture competition, but in the future it could also address a much wider public. The intentions of the Solomon R. Guggenheim Foundation and the city of Vilnius seem to be complementary: A new architectural icon should enhance the importance of the Guggenheim Foundation in the art scene, extend its reach with a new location in Europe, and at the same time put the town, which will be the European Capital of Culture in 2009, "on the market."

Wide public interest in contemporary architecture has also been raised by a series of buildings, i.e., the Elbphilharmonie in Hamburg by Herzog & de Meuron, the Blur Building at the Expo 2002 on Lake Neuchatel by Diller & Scofidio, the Mercedes-Benz Museum in Stuttgart by UN Studio, the Santa Caterina Market in Barcelona by EMBT, the Metropol Parasol in Seville by Jürgen Mayer H., or the Selfridges store in Birmingham by Future Systems. All of these buildings are architectural statements beyond technical and spatial innovation. The experience that people (will) have when visiting these buildings can be described as similar to the spatial experience people had in earlier ages when visiting a church or cathedral. With the shift of our Western society from a religious to a leisure society, linked with the general shift of the major amount of the money from the church to the private sector, the modern "cathedrals" of our time are palaces for cultural events, leisure and shopping. Charles Jencks has stated that the iconic building is the modern cathedral. He has pointed out that a building like the Selfridges store in Birmingham "has appropriated the position of the church, both literally and metaphorically," with a façade "like a garrulous matron at a cocktail party." The cathedral stands for the incorporation of people's belief in contemporary powers, so to speak. Today, business and lifestyle often come before religion. Even though religion has kept its power for parts of our society, a broader public bases their belief on non-religious concerns. In the same sense, modern icons are non-religious and are instead part of our cultural and economic world.

right
Santa Caterina Market
Barcelona, Spain
Architects: EMBT

below
Mercedes-Benz Museum
Stuttgart, Germany
Architects: UN Studio

The relevance of images in POP architecture

Semiotics is an approach to communication through objects, the image of the objects and their interpretation. Architectural semiotics is linked to the history of building science and part of our traditional understanding of architecture. Today we (re-)discuss the phenomenon of semiotic space and iconic architecture on multiple levels.

POP architecture operates as a series of complex mechanisms and one of the most important of these mechanisms is semiotics.

On the one hand the icon embodies the introduction of sculptural stand-alone objects in our cities, which work as mass attractions. On the other hand, the icon reestablished itself in our society as a branding tool to be used by the global markets. The production and reproduction of striking, characteristic, and legible images generate memorable pictures of our environment. In this sense, iconic architecture is POP architecture, and is potentially capable of producing multiple identities for the masses. Yet another aspect of semiotics is interesting when interrogating POP architecture: While the construction of buildings takes a long time, production of the images of these future buildings is fast. What interests the public in the first place is the image that stays present in their mind while the architecture, the building itself, is still produced on-site.

Iconic architecture has its roots in the philosophy of semiotics, a term that is often linked to ornamental architecture or the architecture of the spectacular, and therefore has developed negative connotations. Vicki Goldberg refers to semiotics as "(...) the discipline which seeks to determine the structure of forms by interpreting the societal role of signs and symbols." Applied to the critical analysis and discourse concerning our everyday life, semiotics provides a path towards the active envisioning of messages. As discussed earlier, a constant characteristic of POP culture is the fact that it claims a triumphal return of the object and image, and that it functions through borrowing an iconography directly from daily life of mass culture. To further analyze and discuss semiotics, reference must be made to Roland Barthes, a French philosopher who investigated the deeper understanding of language through nonverbal signs. He claimed that society is a construction, perpetuated by signs of the dominant values within its culture. One of his research fields was bourgeois society. Through his investigations he noted that cultural myths were often founded on signs, e.g., the wine bottle, which, in the 20th century, was a symbol of wealth and a healthy and relaxing lifestyle. While the long-established meaning of wine incorporated foremost the danger of alcohol, the bourgeoisie defined a new image of

Eiffel Tower
Paris, France

wine with a limited and segregated definition purely linked to their lifestyle. With this redefinition of an image, the broader understanding of this beverage changed over time and became an important attribute for a particular social class. While previously the bottle of wine had represented a dangerous lifestyle, the bourgeois society changed its image to one of a luxurious and healthy lifestyle. Semiotics is thus not only an instrument for envisioning information, but it also carries influential factors as the possibility for easy idealization and metaphoric interpretations.

Roland Barthes points out that the reading and understanding of our city cannot only work through "functional studies" but also through the visual significance. He researches the Eiffel Tower in Paris and concludes that it attracts prominence in the way "a lightning rod attracts thunderbolts." The Eiffel Tower is a monument to which our society has attached meaning from the very beginning. While Gustave Eiffel justified the construction of the tower in terms of usability, others linked its meaning primarily to its symbolic value. The tower today is a monument and a symbol for Paris, or even France. During the construction of the Eiffel Tower in 1886, Guy de Maupassant was a sharp critic. He called the tower a "high and skinny pyramid of iron ladders, this giant ungainly skeleton upon a base that looks built to carry a colossal monument of Cyclops, but which just peters out into a ridiculous thin shape like a factory chimney." Maupassant belonged to a group of several representatives of literature and the arts that described the Eiffel Tower as a threat to historical Paris, as a folly, or even a new "Tower of Babel." He understood the aesthetics of the Eiffel Tower as linked to the new technical engineering of the times and as a humiliation to all other monuments in Paris. In the end, such critiques of the Eiffel Tower were lost in a triumphant opening at the World's Fair in 1889. In light of enormous popular success, the Eiffel Tower became a new universal symbol for Paris, with two million visitors during the duration of the World's Fair. Remarkably enough, its importance did not diminish, but grew over time. Maupassant continued to oppose the new monument in the city of Paris. And as the Eiffel Tower was the highest structure in Paris it had a visual omnipresence in the city. To escape from this image he often lunched at the restaurant in the tower, saying that it was "the only place in Paris where I don't have to see it."

"Eiffel Tower"
Hotel *Paris Las Vegas*, Las Vegas, USA

Today, the Eiffel Tower has not lost any of its importance. It is one of or maybe even *the* major sign for a whole country. As Barthes states, it "touches the most general human image repertoire: its simple, primary shape confers upon it the vocation of an infinite cipher." As both lookout point and visually omnipresent monument in Paris, the Eiffel Tower is able to transgress the phenomena of seeing and being seen. Even though this monument is empty, it receives twice as many visitors as the Louvre. The tower becomes a spectacle that everybody wants to experience, even though there is no clear explanation, despite the longing for the spectacular.

Looking at Las Vegas, an enormous replica of the Eiffel Tower is situated right in front of the hotel *Paris Las Vegas*. While the hotel *New York New York*, just a few meters away on the strip of Las Vegas, uses the whole skyline of the City of New York (and not only, e.g., the Statue of Liberty) as recognizable attribute, the Eiffel Tower becomes the major indicator for the *Paris Las Vegas*. With this being identified, it becomes apparent that there is a series of rules for the application of semiotics, and that the example of the Eiffel Tower shows clearly that one aspect of these rules is common sense, or the opinion of the people. Even though avant-garde thinking did not want to allow the addition of another symbolic monument to the city of Paris, the Eiffel Tower became *the* popular icon for the city.

Rethinking POP art, the discovery of the iconography of everyday life – the consumer products, the items of our leisure society, the advertisement, the comic strip, the movies, and the stills – has been essential. Despite aspiring to superficial mass acceptance, POP art had and has a subversive undertone. The combination of reality and art critiques the predominant consumer culture, but also opposes the idea that art is an elitist phenomenon. POP art acquired vogue and spread much faster than any artistic movement before it, and POP artists seeing themselves as bohemians were elevated to stardom. Even though we are observing an "iconic turn" (Gottfried Boehm, 1994) in architecture today, POP art pointed out the dominance of the simulacrum long before.

Hence, can we claim iconic architecture to be POP architecture? And are the architects designing and constructing these buildings called POP stars? What is the potential and what is the danger within these categorizations?

The Eiffel Tower is not understood as a POP building, but can rather be described as a constructed utopian proposal, linked to the intellectual class and the technical development of that time. Nevertheless, it incorporates the primary longing for an architecture of the fantastic, and therefore an essential aspect of POP architecture. Furthermore, with its straightforward semiotics, it is omnipresent in popular culture. It is the background for art, literature, film, music, fashion, and important cultural events. And its small-scale reproductions are mass-consumed by tourists. Having visited the Eiffel Tower is considered as a trophy, and symbolizes a successful visit to Paris. While on the one hand the Eiffel Tower is not considered to be POP architecture, it has on the other hand established a global economy of attention. Like the Eiffel Tower, POP architecture has to not only incorporate accessible semiotics, but to allow for a physical or mental presence in the minds of the general public.

Kunsthaus Graz
Graz, Austria
Architects: Peter Cook and Colin Fournier

An architecture of attention

As mentioned earlier, we now experience an increasing number of politicians and businesspeople constructing icons of power in their cities without hesitation. These buildings explicitly represent an architecture of attention and function as a branding tool, underscoring a corporate identity on the global market through remarkable, extravagant architecture.

Besides the example of the Guggenheim Museum, the design of the Elbphilharmonie in Hamburg, Germany by the Swiss architects Herzog & de Meuron is interesting. The Elbphilharmonie was intended to be a new landmark, and this project has (until now) been a model for a successful business endeavor and a positive city-marketing strategy. The media confront us with never-before-seen images of it, presented and reproduced with an amazing visual force. Through this ongoing media presence, the Elbphilharmonie has established an economy of attention that not only resulted in a wider acceptance of its architecture, but also enabled the city to attract greater financial investments. In conclusion, we can consider the Elbphilharmonie a popular building, as it tries to reach a wider public through eye-catching design and images. But can we consider it a POP building? This discussion of POP phenomena in architecture began by emphasizing the fear of populist architecture, understanding the populist as a person acting from an elitist level, trying to reach the wider population by answering their needs and operating as a precise tactician to lure the masses. Herzog & de Meuron are considered influential avant-garde architects, not operating on a populist level. However, the Elbphilharmonie closes the gap between architects and lay people that was created by the alienations of the Modern Movement. As does the Guggenheim Museum in Bilbao. In both examples, a communication with the population and the user has been established through attractive image design or "imagineering" (as Walt Disney calls it).

"A sa manière, l'image tue" claimed Henri Lefebvre in 1974. Thus, with the privileging of the image, the understanding of space has lost its multi-dimensional capacity, especially in the field of lived experiences. This means that, with the predominance of the image, space is experienced mainly visually. Yet a space can – and should – be experienced with all of the senses. Lefebvre called for a non-codified or non-symbolic approach to space. His argument is clear: The danger of iconic buildings being superficial signs is subliminally present, as in Venturi, Scott Brown and Izenour's "duck." Kenneth Frampton criticizes "architecture that presents itself as exuberantly plastic wherein sculptural concatenations are proffered as the substance of a unprecedented 'value-free' expression." But does a good iconic building necessarily entail bad architecture?

Yet another indication for an architecture of attention and recognition is the creation of nicknames for buildings, a phenomenon which will just briefly be mentioned here. The acceptance of buildings by the wider public through nicknames, alluding to certain characteristics, has a traditional relevance. For example, the congress hall in Berlin has been given the name "Schwangere Auster" ("Pregnant Oyster") by the citizens. This name is linked to the outer appearance of the building, associating its shape with a commonly known object. Today, an intensification of this phenomenon can be distinguished. Recent buildings have received names like "Friendly Alien" (Kunsthaus Graz by Peter Cook and Colin Fournier), "Bird's Nest" (Olympic stadium in Bejing by Herzog & de Meuron), or "The Cloud" (Expo Pavilion in Yverdon-les-Bains by Diller & Scofidio), leaving a positive connotation in peoples' minds, and helping the lay person to memorize buildings in a non-graphical way.

Will this movement today raise again the questions asked by Venturi and Scott Brown, and lead us back to the Strip in Las Vegas and the single family homes of Levittown, or have we come to a point at which architects can take advantage of iconic architecture for a new interaction with and acceptance by society? Could this newly established economy of attention in architecture not imply a positive moment for architects to draw attention to their profession, and profit from it?

E EE 1239

Row houses
Köln, Germany.
Architects: Gruhl Architekten

The exterior appearance talks about the unification of neighboring homes – only the inside leaves room for personal expression.

People's architecture

We can be wrong and we can make mistakes. Since 1970, the biggest mistake that we have made is reading philosophy. Since then, we have been awaiting an answer about how to think and act correctly. All this fight about who is right and who is wrong is boring; full of cowardice.
[Peter Cook]

Zeig mir Deine Wohnung und ich sage Dir, wer Du bist.
[from: Das deutsche Wohnzimmer]

Numerous critics described Modern planning strategies as failures – as did the urbanist Jane Jacobs in *The Death and Life of Great American Cities*, or the psychologist and urban and architectural critic Alexander Mitscherlich in *Our Inhospitable Cities*. Architects such as Archigram or Robert Venturi and Denise Scott Brown, for example, reacted to the Modern Movement in architecture with their explicit studies and designs. Both groups detected a series of dangerous, inhuman facets, and delusional hopes in modernist thinking and planning, and were open to the idea of a "people's architecture." While Archigram used ecstatic and colorful illusions to make proposals linked to everyday lifestyles, Venturi, Scott Brown and Izenour investigated the actual living conditions of the people. Especially in their study of Levittown, they explained the architectural symbolism and ornamentation of the middle class and their longing for social recognition. The "decorated sheds" in Levittown are stereotyped shelters with a predefined architectural repertoire, sold by a series of contractors and individually decorated by the owners with symbolic attributes. This kind of aesthetic of the "banal" represents an architectural language that is commonly understood. It is an iconography that overwrites any "sophisticated architect's" approach.

Mostly ignored today, this domain of POP architecture suggests that architects should accept that many of their clients are not members of an elite or high culture and are not able to adapt to spaces designed by formalistic approaches. That implies that designers need to abandon their elitist position and start engaging in phenomena that have mostly been happening without them, and not close their eyes to mainstream architecture. POP is a feeling, a lifestyle. POP means making the ordinary special. And the (ordinary) personal environment is crucial to a person's lifestyle.

In fact, publicly and privately used spaces have both different potential and requirements to satisfy people's needs. Even though a public building can attract people through its function alone, a private building, such as a family home, might be the most important space for a human being. This is yet another field where POP architecture could result in an explosion of new ways of experiencing space and of living. Architects have rarely been involved in privately built POP architecture as family homes. This market has been dominated by construction companies, providing fairly cheap, often pre-fabricated spaces ready for private decoration. But the process of the appropriation of a space should allow for more than decoration. Architects are (or need to be) able to translate people's thoughts and habits into constructed space, and replace the generic family home with "designed to fit houses." Thus a built space offers shelter from the outside as well as – depending on its designated function – a kind of recognizable feeling or atmosphere.

INTRODUCTION

POP architecture – a polemic

So how can the term "POP architecture" be outlined, and what kind of buildings can be considered POP architecture?

>> POP architecture is reaching the masses
>> POP architecture is giving identity
>> POP architecture is satisfying human needs
>> POP architecture is attractive
>> POP architecture is subversive
>> POP architecture is easy and fast to erect
>> POP architecture is exaggeration
>> POP architecture is transient or adaptive

POP architecture describes buildings that create identities and attract the general public through singular shapes, fascinating materials, or the powerful images they leave in our heads. Furthermore, POP architecture is architecture answering and fulfilling the needs of those using it. And it may even be the low-cost structures of the temporarily erected spaces, such as market places or event locations, designed by (today) non-architects.

Reyner Banham has put it this way: "POP puts the ultimate command in the hands, if not of the consumer, then at least of the consumer's appointed agents." POP architecture of that kind can surely not rely on aesthetic or functional doctrines that avoid inspiration from popular culture. Yet POP architecture does not necessarily lead to a superficialization of our built environment. Architecture, like art, is not compelled to become a non-intellectual low-culture phenomenon, it just has to draw the right conclusions from POP culture. Las Vegas is POP architecture, but POP architecture is not Las Vegas. The same is true for *Disneyland* or suburban family idylls. The occupation with the ostensible "banal and unattractive" can and should inspire architects to an improvement of urban and architectural spaces.

Here, the aspect of public stardom is incorporated, an essentially important aspect of POP culture. As in any field of POP, architects can strive to reach stardom. However, the essence of POP architecture needs to exceed the idea of the general public keeping a replica or photograph of a building, or a poster of the architect, in their living rooms.

Gerd de Bruyn and the IGMA Team describe the contemporary condition of architecture as "Option POP." This option is specified as a chance for the architects to break the spell of the *Baumeistertum* and start understanding their profession as part of our service industry. They describe this service by referring to an expert-laymen model: "Fand der Experte im genialen Dilettanten seinen Spiritus rector, rekrutiert sich der POP-Profi immer wieder aufs Neue aus dem Heer der Amateure, die sein Publikum sind." This "Option POP" in fact will not only include the aesthetic configuration of buildings, but also the marketing strategies of architects. The enhancement of architecture as a service (as opposed to architecture as exclusively the art and science of designing and constructing buildings) raises new issues in our contemporary architectural discourse. Mies van der Rohe's doctrine "As reduced as possible, at all costs" can therefore no longer be a guideline for spatial productions in the era after the Modern Movement.

Accepting and engaging in POP architecture requires architects to rethink, to open up and to accept the confrontation with reality. The outcome can introduce a "POP turn."

A "POP turn," meaning an acceptance of and an involvement in POP architecture, can on the one hand lead to a new engagement of architects in social needs and demands and/or, on the other hand, to an amplification of the predominance of the image, the carrying-on of the "iconic turn," which in this sense would then simply represent the start of an upcoming "POP age."

People want to be popular, and so do architects. But today, first of all, they strive to be popular amongst themselves, to be admired more by their colleagues and critics than by their customers. Architects are taught to do so. And despite all the changes in architectural practice today, it seems to be a problem to admit to being a POP player, a POP lover, or a POP architect. The danger of populism persists and needs to be carefully eliminated. But alienation from the general public is not the answer to avoiding populist tendencies. Rather, a fresh interest in POP phenomena in architecture can open up a new field of possibilities.

So let's figure out what we discern and detect in contemporary mainstream, or at its edges.

top right
Market place in Krakow
Poland

bottom right
WideShut
Architects: XTH-berlin
Prototype for a sensitive façade system. This installation consists of twelve motorized umbrellas that react to changing light conditions.

1 THE PERSONAL IS POP

THIS WAS TOMORROW

Sandra Bartoli

In both principle and situation, POP is dynamic. It is the moment between culture and its destruction, the mob and the hero, Walt Disney and his manic depression. This cognitive feedback loop is electric and illuminating. I'm wonderful. I'm high.

A world of absolute bad faith, where the real and the true are superseded by simulacra and the hyperreal.
[Istvan Csicery-Ronay]

Popular culture is the testbed of our futurity.
[William Gibson]

Kim Jong Il mastermind

Tourists visiting North Korea are always appointed a guide who never leaves his or her side during the visit. The guide's purpose is not only to escort the visitor, but also to filter one's perception of the country. Christian Kracht, Eva Munz and Lukas Nikol describe this phenomenon in their latest book *Total Memory – Kim Jong Il's North Korea* (*Die totale Erinnerung – Kim Jong Il's Nordkorea*), which relates the story of their visit to a film studio.

According to the book, at first, the studio seemed neglected and in disuse; but after a while they were led by their guides to a group of people making a film. There were actors dressed as medieval Korean warriors engaged in a fight scene, the film director was sitting on a big chair, barking orders and smoking; but the scene lights were off, the camera wasn't plugged in, and nobody was filming. Later on, back at the hotel, Kracht, Munz and Nikol watched the evening news on TV. There was a special feature on a group of foreigners visiting a film studio: in the end, they were the ones who had been taped by a hidden video camera during the visit ...

This story depicts a borderline situation in which Kim Jong Il showed that he has learned the POP lesson much too well. One can in this case read the entire country as a gigantic act of illusion and deception.

Popular culture is understood within this context as a time-based phenomenon. It is about touching the edges of reality where things are being shaped and at the same time crumbling.

Time

Popular culture is a time-based phenomenon. And it is also a personal story, in terms of the coruscating youth fights, opposing a status quo, and generational processes; it is highly dynamic. It is about life, death, and sex, or in other words: construction, destruction, and desire. These are the "eternal" categories at the core of the envisioning of different futures. Popular culture becomes a matter of suggestion and persuasion, the material of media efficacy. North Korea represents a very sophisticated example of this script. Under these premises Potsdamer Platz in Berlin can also be seen as a very POP place. In 1991, it was originally conceived within a master plan to create an elite space with references to European urban models such as Florence or Siena; meanwhile, the economic reality determined its existence as a large shopping mall. Ultimately Potsdamer Platz has become an unintentionally ironic "synthespian" of contemporary European culture.

In this way, an examination of popular culture often allows one to decipher where things are leading to, offering the chance to infer the broad strokes of the future and thus to operate directly within its paradigms. Projecting future conditions by adding layers to a given situation is called retrofitting. This is a superficial (i.e., surface-based) process that builds on an existing context, in terms of inventing new programs and adding infrastructures, as well as instruments and architectural decorum. Thus, research on futures has become a process of surface layering. This acceleration of envisioning new realities can be incremented by the adoption of a slipstream attitude. Slipstream, as Bruce Sterling describes it, is a contemporary kind of writing, or better, a creative attitude, which tears at the structure of "everyday life." He continues, saying that "frequently, historical figures are used in slipstream fiction in ways which outrageously violate the historical record. History, journalism, official statements, advertising copy ... all of these are grist for the slipstream mill, and are disrespectfully treated not as 'real-life facts' but as 'stuff,' raw material for collage work. These are fantastic elements which are not clear-cut departures from known reality but ontologically understood as a 'part of the whole mess'."

As the most commonly accepted starting point for POP culture, the 1960s can be perceived as a euphoric moment for a tremendous convergence of desire: fashion, music, new ways for people to aggregate, live, and love: the thriving of subculture altogether. This same moment was also a moment of struggle, where people were suffering from so much repression that they started to rebel on every level, from the personal to the public: everything is political.

And things went bad: the Vietnam war, the Nixon administration, the repression within the family, the police harassment of anybody who showed opposition to convention, the hypocrisy of the education system, etc. This was a time of great tension that led to radical change. It wasn't only a hedonistic moment portrayed in what is widely known as "POP." It became a revolution.

Today it has become clear that the whole revolution thing can also be seen as a very effective process – partly organized bottom-up, partly top-down, where the marketing of POP products for new consumer target groups – mostly young people with money – meets the desires of these people. Thus the '60s, in this interpretation, were an enormous reform boost for capitalist society. It permanently tries to destroy traditions and the strict organization of society to create a class whose main purpose is consumption. The flip side of rebellion and emancipation is the liberation of its subjects to consume new kinds of lifestyles.

One of the most important and influential books released during this time was *The Whole Earth Catalog – Access to Tools*, by Stewart Brand. This was the first universal do-it-yourself manual which taught how to do everything, from building a geodesic structure to providing sensual massages to a lover. A hip book for alternative societies, independent and self-empowered. Steve Jobs in 2005 during his commencement speech at Stanford University compared this catalog to an information sourcing book, a conceptual proto search-engine.

Hydrogen Bomb
Mushroom cloud from US nuclear test "Castle Bravo," Bikini Atoll, March 1st, 1954

Grandma Vivienne
with Coocoo, Nika and David, Gstaad, 1965

Futurity

"Popular culture is the testbed of our futurity," as William Gibson tells us in *Idoru*. In all his work Gibson subliminally suggests with magical clarity that enough attention to things POP is a way to recognize the moment of change in our collective consciousness, which is a change of meaning and not simply a change in style.

This means that the understanding and production of POP values is fundamental to the discipline of architecture, which encompasses all the built world, and doesn't restrict itself to becoming a discipline of elitism and denial. If resistance is worthless then there must be an intelligent way of affirming POP culture.

Potsdamer Platz
Berlin, Germany, 2006

THE GARDEN OF EARTHLY DELIGHTS

Anna Hyyppä, Hege I.R. Schjønhaug

The term "POP" is linked to the ideas of something easily accessible, attractive, fast to produce, convenient, and mainstream, not high class and exclusive. *The Garden of Earthly Delights* is an artificial outdoor resort using the landscape to attract people. You can enjoy a down-to-earth experience while an invisible high-tech machine provides all necessary supplies. *The Garden of Earthly Delights* is POP because you can't go wrong: There are always fish in the pond, leaves to rake in the hills, and the BBQ in the valley is always perfect. The resort provides everything you need and everyone will have the feeling of success over and over again.

We were trying to find a way to make life simpler but not less interesting. We wanted to offer people new free time activities other than buying and consuming, using the primitive need of man to get in touch with nature.

Our approach

We were interested in the hyper-consumption of today and tomorrow, and wanted to find alternatives to that horror image of humankind. We had the golden opportunity to use more than 1000 square meters of land, therefore we were determined to use the whole site. We wanted to work more with landscape instead of a single building.

POP in the landscape

Most people want to go out in the open air. This need has different aspects in cities where the connection to nature is not an everyday thing. Parks and gardens are the only places to feel and use nature; therefore landscape and park planning are especially important in cities. City life is fast and busy, going directly from A to B. When you hit a park, time stops for a while. You can rest and forget your stress for a moment. Nature and free air are connected to the idea of a healthy and "fresh" life. Thus, nature is popular among both busy city inhabitants and more slow paced country people. Thus, nature can be seen as POP – in this case meaning popular – as can the landscape. For this reason, architecture uses the landscape to make itself POP. *The Garden of Earthly Delights* uses the landscape and other natural elements to attract people and become a place loved by the citizens of Berlin.

Program

The Garden of Earthly Delights is an artificial outdoor resort with a blanket of grass covering the whole site. The resort consists of six outside activity areas covering a large, underground service infrastructure. You will enter through *The Arrival Gate*, walk past *The House of Culinary Sensations*, continue your way down in *The Valley of the BBQ*, join the happy people in *The Garden of Raking*, take a short dip in *The Pond of Recreation*, and end up in *The Village in the Woods*. The resort combines the easy and simple life above with the service and consumption machine below. You have the opportunity to enjoy down-to-earth experiences outside while the machine underneath keeps the resort alive.

The Garden of Earthly Delights responds to the human need to go back to nature and do some work with one's own hands. Its social importance lies in offering people an escape from consumerism.

Urban context

The Garden of Earthly Delights provides a service to the wider public. It's a new free time alternative for city people without their own backyard and garden. In fact, *The Garden* functions as a new plug-in to the city. It is strong in its visual presence and has clear edges. The existing conditions and height levels in the site are completely changed, and *The Garden* differs strongly from the urban area around it. It blends into the city only in the high-rise area on the eastern edge.

The atmosphere inside the resort gives a feeling of being somewhere else. The Nordbahnhof site is easily accessed by public transportation. The main entrance, being close to Invalidenstrasse, gives *The Garden* visibility from the busiest traffic area. *The Garden* can be accessed from most of the streets around it and can be used also for passing through.

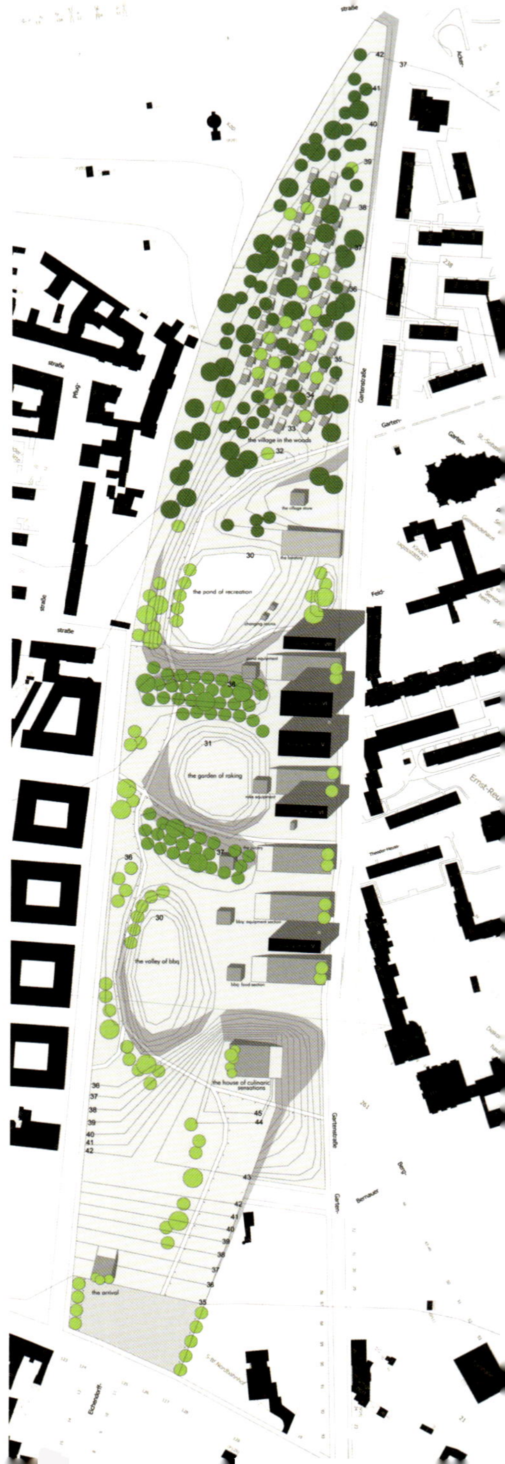

Architecture, economy, and media

In terms of architectural form and design, the garden part is the focus. Grass covers and hides most of the building mass. In the resort area only small pieces of the mass are visible, creating a rural and quiet atmosphere. The little stores and some major points like the restaurant and main entrance info box are clearly visible, hinting at the things going on underneath. The high-rises along Gartenstrasse stand out and respond to the city around. A clear division between client use and private use is part of *The Garden*. The maintenance function is strictly hidden and out of sight. The clients are supposed to be fully served but in a discrete way. A big part of the inner circulation goes through the machine part underneath the resort. In the upper resort area the path works as a main way through *The Garden* and leads people on the journey.

The economic concept is mainly based on the commercial outlets for garden equipment. The mixed use of offices and housing in the high-rises provide a range of possibilities to finance the resort.

The Garden of Earthly Delights has a clear identity as an artificial resort for down-to-earth activities. There is a strong narrative and storyline to the resort. The iconography of *The Garden* plays an important role in creating this narrative. The small icons for every activity spot, as well as the signs and maps along the path, help orientate visitors. Regionally, *The Garden* serves as a leisure resort for both tourists and local city people. It works as a tourist attraction in the functional and usable way, not as a sight itself. People don't come over to take pictures, they come to participate.

left
Site plan
with *The Arrival Gate* in the south and the remote *Village in the Woods* in the north

below
The machine
covered by *The Garden*

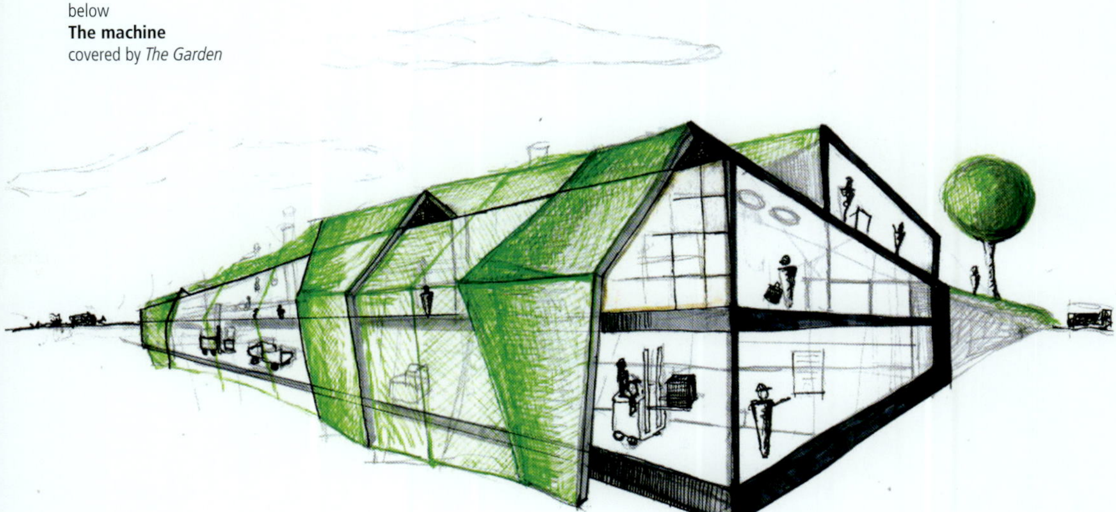

The machine and the garden

The Garden of Earthly Delights is a combination of the easy, simple life above and the service and consumption machine below. While you enjoy quiet life outside, the machine underneath keeps the resort alive. Everything happens very fast under the surface. The action above never stops and the machine is at all times up and running. Since *The Garden* is in the middle of the city, people don't have to leave their normal lives to go there.

Leo Marx is one of those who have made deeper researched views of the machine in the garden and the basic human need to go back to nature. Marx writes about the "pastoral ideal," the rural, romantic, and agrarian myth, or the myth of the garden in some cases. Pastoralism is the idyllic portrayal of a place away from the city. Marx based his research into pastoralism and machine age mostly on literary sources. He looks into the way machines were portrayed symbolically in American literature, and writes about the contradiction between the pastoral ideal and the growing technological machine culture. In this process, the transition from the early North American farm life to the modern machine-age reflects the movement from a rural lifestyle to urban city

Street
Perspective collage

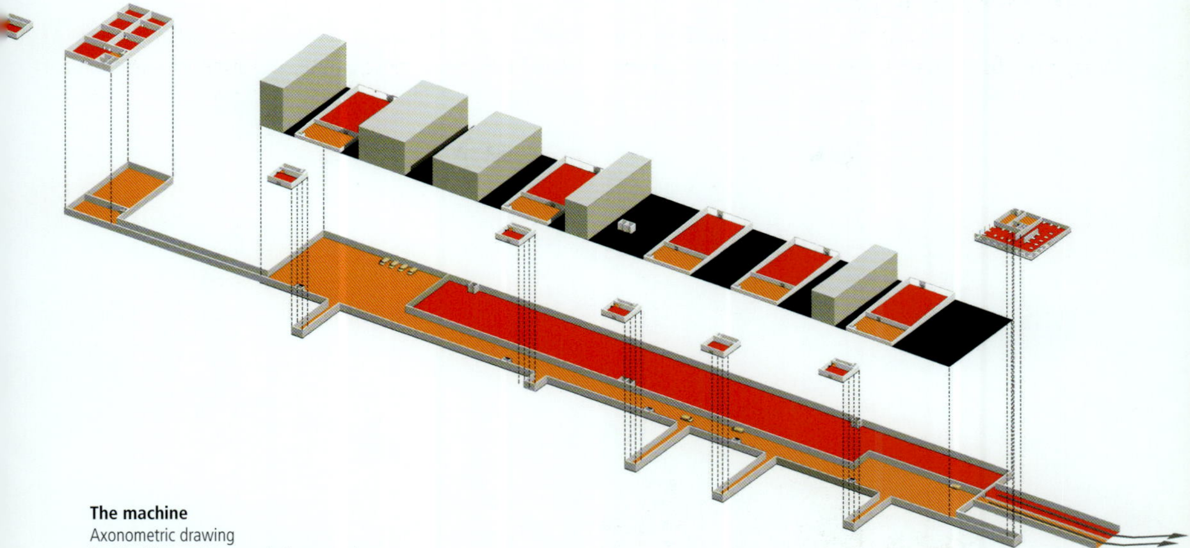

The machine
Axonometric drawing
Red (public zone), orange (private zone)

living. The question of this process is what kind of sacrifices in the pastoral life are to be made in order to achieve technological progress. To Leo Marx, the machine is the metaphor for industrialization in America. "The general faith was that things were going to get better and better – not only materially but also morally, politically, and socially – and this predominant view assumed that advancing technology was a sufficient basis for that progress," wrote Marx in 1988. The idea of progress was not dependent on faith but on reason, science, and technology, the works of man himself.

Marx contrasts this concept of machine-power progress with the Jeffersonian-American ideal of pastoralism – illustrated by the garden metaphor. "There was a belief that we could resolve our deepest problems by building a simpler world combining the best of art and nature," he writes. Marx's thoughts illustrate the process where American public life may be defined as a struggle between two types of progress: the machine and the garden.

Thomas Jefferson also commented on the problem of wanting to live the simple life on a farm surrounded by nature, and still having to exist in a civilized society filled with machinery, industrialism, and technology. A crucial part of the pastoral ideal is the early colonial movement from the primitive forest to cultivated land. It has within itself the contradiction between taming wild nature, but at the same time not exploiting the natural resources to the point of sterility and alienating the farmer from his environment. In this movement from nature to nurture, the machine or technology is not an enemy, as long as we use it in a balanced and sustainable manner. "Mankind must depart from the state of nature – but not too far," as Jean Jacques Rousseau wrote about early American pastoral life.

19th and early 20th century movements like Romanticism and the Arts and Crafts Movement, in addition to the Garden City Movement and postwar suburbs, look into the popular notion of the pastoral garden.

The Valley of the BBQ
The perfect place for BBQs and picnics

The rural landscape in the 19th and early 20th century movements was thought of as a new version of nature, neither a wild untamed force nor a cold scientific creation.

To those movements, the pastoral garden, rather than the machine-city, was essential in rediscovering spiritualism in public life. J.H. Kunstler points out that "it was a safe, green, warm, sheltering, life-giving realm, full of fruit, grains, flocks of sheep and fowl, its hills and valleys feminine in their voluptuousness and ability to nurture. It was a sweet homeland, at last." And most of all, it was the opposite of the new place called the industrial city. The social contract between the garden and the machine can be seen in the striving for "good life." The goal of both modern high-tech society and idyllic rural culture is to achieve a satisfactory way of living, only the means to reach it differ. In modern society man still feels some kind of connection with nature. Whenever city people want to "get away from it all," they choose back-to-nature vacations by going camping, hiking, and sunbathing on the seashore. Enjoying the garden is a balance between man as a part of nature and man as a dominator of nature.

The artificial garden in the city

For this reason, *The Garden of Earthly Delights* is everyday and mainstream POP, not high class and exclusive POP. People are fed up with the fake and glossy things, now they go for the real thing: the artificial resort. *The Garden* did not grow at the Nordbahnhof all by itself; rather, it was planned with great attention to detail to work perfectly as an enjoyable resort. Nothing is left to coincidence: The resort functions around the clock, and its customers are always well served. They just don't notice it themselves while enjoying the perfect green garden that has been built to cover the engine.

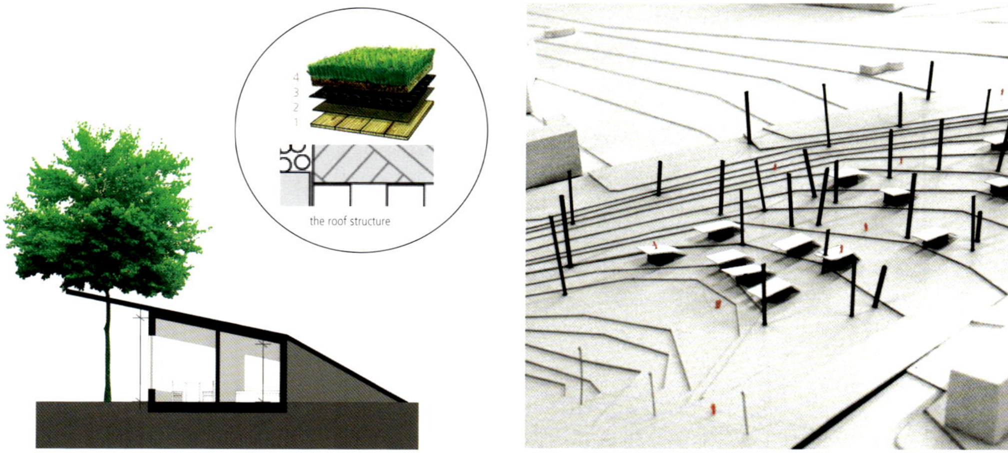

The Village in the Woods
Section of a hut, roof detail, and set-up of the village

There is a tradition of faking it in landscape, from Renaissance gardens all over Europe to English landscape gardens. With the beginning of POP in the 1960s, a new era of fake was born.

Contemporary landscape architects used the fascinating atmosphere of Warhol's POP-driven decade. Landscape architects such as Martha Schwartz, Ken Smith, and West 8 use the same phenomenon in their work.

Martha Schwartz's projects range from private to urban scale. Her background is in the fine arts as well as landscape architecture. The use of her materials originated from an interest in POP art. Schwartz designs with the idea that it is better to offend someone than to do something mediocre, it is better to create something that fascinates for a short time and is cared for than a long-term design that no-one cares about. Schwartz is interested in the use of everyday objects as a way to reject the mainstream. She works with extreme colors, different scales, and glorification of everyday materials. This abstract artistic approach causes controversy as to what landscape really is. She has worked with outrageous concepts to bring humor to design.

By contrast, Ken Smith strives to challenge the distinction between landscape and art form. Smith's MoMA rooftop garden, designed in 2005, is an extreme example of fake gardens. It's not physically accessible: it's a garden for looking at, not a garden for being in. Smith's POP garden presents itself as an oasis of artificiality. It denies any seasonal change, and is uninterested in the fact that it is hyper-real. It is the perfected art of exaggeration with perfectly manicured lawn.

West 8 observes that contemporary landscape is for the most part artificial, made up of different components, designed and undesigned. This allows them the freedom of responding with their own narrative. They want to work in a playful, optimistic manner and take possession of a space. Their philosophy is strongly based on an optimistic attitude towards the contemporary landscape, which expresses both the vulnerability and the euphoria of mass culture. They want to emphasize the contradiction between the organized world of commerce, functionality, and efficiency, and the wasteland spaces of uncertainty and coincidence without a strong identity. West 8 mixes built areas, façades, and vegetation to create surreal botanic structures. To them, gardens are closed and withdrawn from the world, places where people can literally retreat into themselves.

Conclusion

POP depends on the place, the time, and the person looking at it. It is also a question of taste. There cannot be one unequivocal explanation of POP itself. In architecture, it can mean attractive, inviting, or easily accessible. Often it can be as superficial as an outstanding form, shape, or color. We picked out one type of POP that we felt was a bit forgotten, the "simple POP." As a result, *The Garden of Earthly Delights* was made to make people feel good about themselves. It is a reminder of the less complicated, but nevertheless important things in life. *The Garden* uses landscape and natural elements to attract people. It introduces a kind of POP in architecture and landscape design which is not unknown, yet in a new way seductive, as it is subtly satisfying – unconscious – human needs.

View of the resort
offering a glimpse of the city in the background

PUREPLUS LIFE

Sybille Paulsen, Karen Rose

Welcome to your *brand* new world! *PurePlus Life* is a lifestyle community located in the heart of Berlin. Initiated by the Swiss water supplier *PurePlus*, it provides a healthy everyday life based on the positive aspects of *PurePlus* water. A typology is created around three types of housing which seek to maximize this quality. They are arranged around small spa islands floating in an artificial water basin covering the whole site. A day spa offers a taste of the *PurePlus Life* for the public. Architecture no longer serves as a mere "selling room" but as a physical experience of that lifestyle. Already influencing each detail of our everyday life, our lifestyle community is the ultimate spatial phenomenon in marketing, where architecture gives people what they want.

Maximized water experience
A maximized water experience has been created by flooding the site.

PUREPLUS – generating lifestyle, generating homes, generating people

We at *PurePlus* are driven by two desires. First, we seek to create lifestyles centered on *PurePlus* water, and second, we seek to create an architecture which houses these lifestyles. Thus, spatial design becomes our marketing strategy, following a trend that has evolved over the years. Brands create strong and omnipresent images that accompany people deep into their private life.

You, our costumers, are offered the perfect life at *PurePlus* – the same one that you see every day on the TV screen! We, as an ambitious Swiss water supplier, aim to cross the border of being merely a supplier. We aim to create a deeper identification with our brand. Based on the brand philosophy we have filtered out a target group which served as a model for the housing typology. With the design and organization of private, public and community spaces we want to provide you with all necessities and amenities for a harmonious lifestyle.

Before, suburban residential neighborhoods answered most family needs. Today, with *PurePlus Life* we introduce a living comfort and an environment in the inner city of Berlin that is giving you what the outskirts have given you before – *plus* more. With the architecture of *PurePlus Life* we bring your lifestyle dreams to downtown Berlin and invite you to live your dreams!

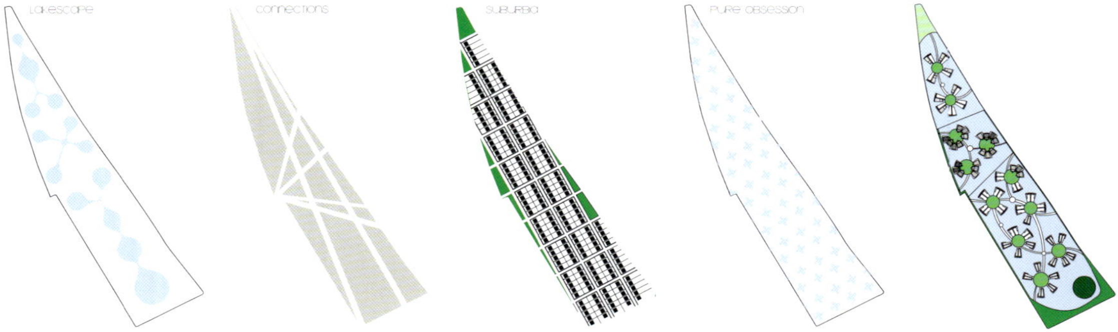

The site

The final site arrangement is a hybrid dominated by round-shaped islands that are surrounded by a water basin stretching over the whole site. Different uses, densities and zones of privacy coexist in an open field.

Parts of the islands stay accessible to the public. The more lively southern part of the site invites the public to enjoy the waterfront with cafés, a promenade, and seating possibilities. The northern part of the site is calmer and therefore ideal for a more private, exclusive area. The shoreline is the "natural" division and the connection between the *PurePlus Life* and the city.

PurePlus residents form a coherent community and the architecture of *PurePlus Life* supports this feeling of coherence. The generator for this concept was an analysis of community life. Believing that the smallest unit in a social collective is not the family but the individual, we developed a scheme to arrange communities in a more functional way. Thus, *PurePlus* living spaces are organized into small, internally connected "islands." The surfaces of the islands are small parks accessible for the people living in the community as well as the public. Housing units are arranged around the parks, only accessible for the residents of course. The entrance floor of the houses is always equipped with public space like living rooms and kitchens. Downstairs the more private areas like bedrooms and bathrooms are situated. A pool in the middle of the house connects the housing unit with the lower level of the park islands, creating space for a community spa. Here, residents of different houses can come together and share the experience of *PurePlus Life*.

While gated communities are built more and more frequently, architectural discourse has not yet addressed this kind of typology. The architecture of *PurePlus Life* is attracting and linking people to a brand and can therefore be considered POP architecture. It is POP because it gives people what they want and tries to fit the taste of many.

But nevertheless PurePlus Life is not regarded as trashy or cheap. Rather, it is exclusive and singular. A villa on the water or an apartment overlooking the artificial lake is the selling idea for the image of PurePlus.

All *PurePlus* residents will identify with their homes. The buildings become the icon for an ideal and popular lifestyle. Architecture has turned POP.

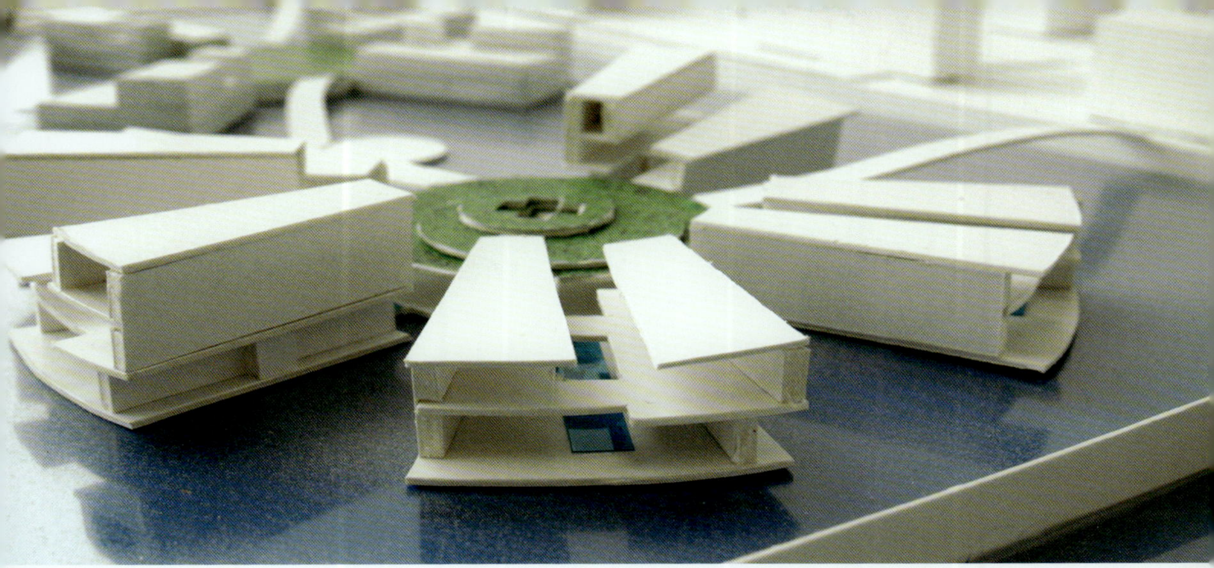

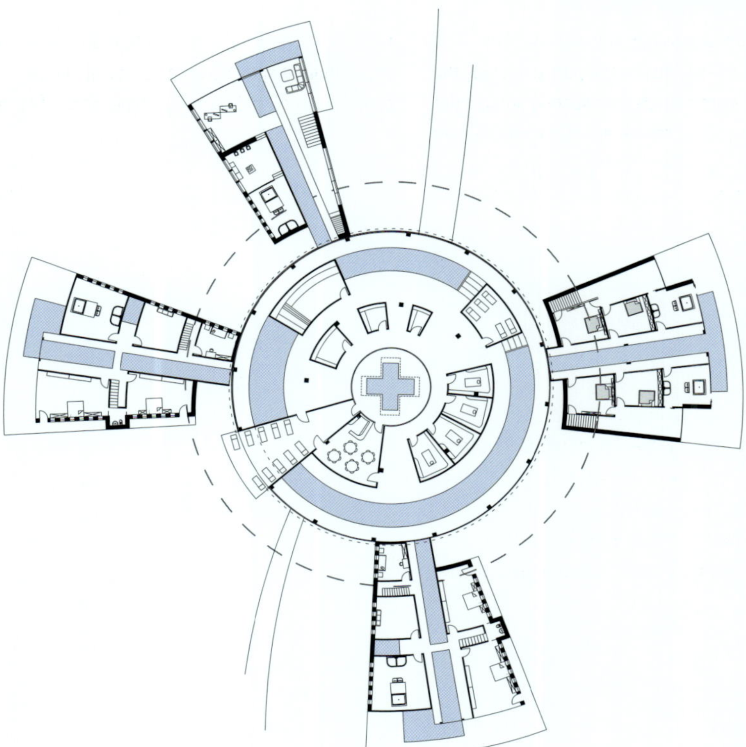

Model and ground floor plan of a *PurePlus* living unit

2 PEOPLE'S POP

WHEN DENISE WAS "LEARNING FROM POP"

Valéry Didelon

ARBEITSAMT

Ben Reynolds

SELECTED – THE NEW EXPERIENCE OF CONSUMPTION

Kalina Aleksandrova, Julie Hoffmann

WHEN DENISE WAS "LEARNING FROM POP"

Valéry Didelon

Learning from POP is the title of an article written by the American architect Denise Scott Brown and published in the Italian magazine *Casabella* in December 1971. Denise Scott-Brown saw POP as popular culture, and she was interested in the question of what architects could (or should) learn from popular culture. The theme was later developed in *Learning from Las Vegas*, a book co-authored with Robert Venturi and Steven Izenour. This question – and its subsequent answer – initiated a major controversy at the time, one which still holds a great deal of interest for us today.

Controversy

There are two main implications to the "Learning from POP" argument. First, it carries the idea that architects should look at popular culture to renew their own culture. As Denise Scott Brown and Robert Venturi said, "to find our symbolism we must go to the suburban edges of the existing city that are symbolically rather than formalistically attractive and represent the aspirations of almost all, including most ghetto dwellers and most of the silent white majority. Then the archetypal Los Angeles will be our Rome and Las Vegas our Florence; and like the archetypal grain elevator some generations ago, the Flamingo sign will be the model to shock our sensibilities towards a new architecture." Second, it makes clear that there is a growing divide between "architects" and "people." In *Casabella*, Denise Scott Brown wrote, "high-style architects are not producing what people want or need." For her, the establishment had cut itself off from the people's expectations. "There is an irony in the fact that the 'popular' culture and the 'popular' landscape are not popular with those who make the decisions to renew the city and rehouse the poor." This charge is aimed directly at the heirs of the Modern Architecture Movement who, according to Scott Brown and Venturi, are intended to build for Man rather than for men.

In the early '70s, this polemical argument brought immediate comments. In an article published in 1974 in *Oppositions*, Fred Koetter stated, "we should help people to get what they want, rather than impose upon them what we think they should have." He also raised even more questions: "Is this really what people want? Do people ever really get what they want, want what they get, or should they?" In the same issue where Denise Scott Brown pleated for learning from POP, the British historian and critic Kenneth Frampton reacted in a virulent way: "Do designers really need elaborate sociological ratification à la Gans, to tell them that what the people want is what they already have?"

Signs of Life: Symbols in the American City. Exhibition in 1976
Venturi, Scott Brown and Associates

In consequence, he includes Scott Brown and Venturi in the American school of "populist urbanism." As he said, "the implicit attitude of this school remains one in which the design professions are to be reactivated only through greater conformity to the sacrosanct populist goals of our affluent society." In his mind, and for many architects and critics at this time, learning from POP was equated with a populist stance.

Denise Scott Brown replied frankly to theses charges. Interviewed in a magazine she confessed the approach:
AMC: Would you prefer the adjective "populist" rather than "POP?"
D.S.B.: In some ways, I prefer even if it carries restricted political meanings; it describes narrow-minded racists and religious people ... Regarding our moral and democratic aspiration, we've got populist leanings.

But while Scott Brown and Venturi were recognizing that they are populist, some reviewers turned it upside down and blamed them for elitism: "Like British POP art, Venturi's work is elitist, not vernacular." The art critic Franz Schulze explained this reversal thusly," ... Venturi's rejection of utopian order and his willingness to 'accommodate to what people do' are not so much populist ideas as they are cryptoaristocratic, for in populist ideas there is no room for keenly sophisticated ironies, sardonic subtleties and mannerist perversities." In a book published at the time, the architect Robert Goodman denounced Robert Venturi for speaking to other architects, and not to the people: "For all of Venturi's rhetoric about the 'experience of life and the needs of society,' his theory is a classic example of elitism. It is in the tradition of one architect producing a theory for the consumption of other architects and critics. It speaks to the tastemakers rather than to the needs of people." In this way, Scott Brown and Venturi were charged with two contradictory arguments. On the one hand, they were blamed for following the conservative goals of the middle class. And, on the other hand, some people reproached them for being too sophisticated and deeply elitist. Once again, Scott Brown and Venturi endorsed the anathema and confessed: "We are elitists, and much of the time we design for an elite market whether we like it or not." Caught between populism and elitism, Denise Scott Brown claimed the role of go-between: "I would say that we are taking a very broadly based thing, which is the popular culture ... and we're trying to make it acceptable to an elitist subculture, namely, the architects and the corporate and governmental decision makers who hire architects."

Understanding

Two insights can actually shed some light on this controversy – one relates populism to the architecture field, and the other to politics.

In architecture, there is a specific understanding of populism, which concerns the de-centering of academic figures. One can identify two main currents of populism in 20th century architecture. According to Jean-Louis Cohen, the first one has to do with the "reclaiming of vernacular forms, often excluded from academic works." It is the idea of "renovating" the architecture culture out of the everyday culture. The second has to do with "people's participation in architectural production," sometimes implemented as advocacy planning – there learning from POP becomes learning from people. There, as Alexander Tzonis said, "the user was to become, for the populist, the official mentor, if not master, of the design decision. In spite of whether a particular proponent of populist architecture favored the low brow and popular visual expression on the strip, or the implementation of user participation and self-help design in the slums, he urged, in all cases, that the design process should be carried out 'in the name of the people'."

In politics, populism is nowadays known as a tendency which pretends to defend ordinary people by fighting against the institutions, the establishment, and the traditional political mediations. In the USA, since the end of 19th century, populism was a left-wing privilege. Defending the ordinary people was the duty of the Democratic Party (especially during the New Deal). But during the sixties, the young radicals of the New Left blamed the "power structure," or the "power elite" for promoting a corporate liberalism which favored the wealthy. They clamored for a participatory democracy, one which would better defend the interests of poor people and the minorities. But more significantly, at the same time populism was migrating from the left to the right side of political agenda. More and more politicians stood up, aiming to defend the interests of the real people, the conservative white workers and employees, who were living in the suburbs. Richard Nixon was thus elected in 1968 as the president of that silent majority. Since that time, populism has been related to far right politics.

Within this context it is easier to understand why the *Learning from POP* stance has been so brutally attacked. Due to its relation to the silent white majority's expectations, Scott Brown and Venturi and their works were classified as elite-populist, or, worse, as "Nixonist" by some critics. *Learning from POP* was thus seen as a right-wing and conservative argument, and the architects who promoted it as conservative persons.

Today, "Learning from POP" is a rather different thing. It has more to do with learning from POP Art, or learning from POP culture as a kind of second-hand learning. To go back to the original debate is in this way quite stimulating. Perhaps it could be seen as a way to re-establish a more engaged, passionately political and relevant position, one which is sadly so often lacking in the architectural field today.

ARBEITSAMT

Ben Reynolds

On the dichotomy of POP

My position is based on an outline of two of the numerous ways of interpreting the word "POP." One, is formed by a fabricated summation by the one in power (i.e., the artist) and aims to receive public admiration, it is normally based on images and a surface acknowledgment. This can indeed connect with people, however, as merely an attraction from a visual. The other interpretation is channeled in the thoughts administered by the people. It intends to reflect the needed quotations. There is no right or wrong answer, however the latter is generally rooted in the considered, calculated and personal. In essence, one is a comment *for* people and the other a comment *by* people. In this case these referrals are positioned in the framework of the individual as a collective, rather than the autonomous. This text aims to profile the work of artists and thinkers who adopt the latter opinion. The resultant architecture – the *Arbeitsamt* – too, is spawned from this rationale, dealing with the context of a *needed* POP building in Berlin.

In the rationalization of the two methods described, one can draw similarities between them. Both are based on the rudimentary human need to create, and also, as outlined in Maslow's *Hierarchy of Needs* for one's own self-actualization, it serves people's instinctual need to make the most of their abilities and to strive to be the best they can. Perhaps those adopting the first method of production see the output as a source of sustainability. Allowing them a material satisfaction, an increase in status, fame, personal advertising, or masturbation – a method of Edward Bernays' term "Public Relation."

The morals or intentions of a work that, needless-to-say, "comes from the people" contain values that pertain to the benefit of sociological and environmental realms. They are productions that reflect on the human condition.

Reflection is an analysis and serves as societal therapy or counselling. The strongest property of this method of creation is that it is personal and comes from an intention to further one's own understanding, and perhaps stimulate discussion, analysis of its own, and, ideally, further critical creation.

Robert Venturi and Denise Scott Brown

Complexity and Contradiction in Architecture was probably the landmark architectural critique of the late 20th century, a shot actually heard, if not around the world, at least beyond the US shortly after mid-century. It wasn't the first chord of the overture to Postmodernism; that startling sound first came with Ronchamp, when Le Corbusier divested himself of the ideology of public virtue and social progress that sanctified orthodox Modernism. Ronchamp in contrast was a decadent throwback to Gaudí, revealing for all to see that Le Corbusier, the heroic Modernist, was really the same sort of intuitive artist, striving for the same sort of other-worldly realm of fantasy. His left-brained, ideological rationale of the CIAM had been cast aside.

Robert Venturi argued against the purity, clarity, and perhaps the coldness of Modernism. With the publication of *Complexity and Contradiction in Architecture* the two principal branches of Modernism, Functionalism and Rationalism, were overturned as paradigms according to Postmodernist and Deconstructivist readings. He claimed that ornament and historical allusion added a new richness to architecture. As a consequence, a series of Postmodern architects endeavored to reapply ornaments even to economical and minimal buildings; an effort best illustrated by Venturi and Scott Brown's concept of "the decorated shed." Finally, Venturi's writing seemed to seal the fate of Modernism, not merely as a style, but as a modernist ideology. He was complaining that architecture, in the modernist quest for ideological certitude, had become irrelevant – this was a Romantic speaking. Modern architecture had in fact morphed to seek to justify its revolution on theoretical arguments that hoped to make itself acceptable as objective. What Germany got (at that time) was Neue Sachlichkeit, polar to the sentiment of the now-dead Victorians, all sweetness and light, but it was the sentiment of the current popular culture, which was a consumer culture addicted to mass media.

PEOPLE'S POP

What Modernism removed was the charm and comfort common to the Prairie School, Kenneth Frampton's Critical regionalism, Art Nouveau, even the pitiful efforts found in Postmodern architecture, heralded as the return of "wit, ornament, and reference." In a sense Venturi's attempt was a new sort of "Realism," which was anti-elitist, contra those ideological theorists who would tell us what we ought to have and what was good for us.

Alain de Botton

Comparatively, it was the popular contemporary philosopher Alain de Botton who tackled that very question. He saw the power of movements that affect the collective, "it's buildings that probably have the greatest influence on us today: they can literally persuade us to be certain kinds of people." The closest he came to a rational, respectful conclusion was that, "(...) we are drawn to call something successful whenever we detect that it contains in a concentrated form those qualities in which we personally, or our societies more generally, are deficient."

Pleasure or the success of architecture for de Botton can be found in what was personally lacking. Perhaps it is not necessarily the light or shadow a space exhibits, but the mundane: the doorknobs, window mullions, brickwork, and other such architectural paraphernalia. It seems that the way to happiness in architecture resides in our own visual pleasure, the surface treatment, the way we articulate light or the distribution of the material. Venturi was saying that architecture was removed from this phenomenon, that it had become too abstract, too disengaged from the reality of the popular culture, and too elitist in its pedantic ideology that presumed to tell us what was good for us. This was not merely refreshing, but liberating. Of course, he unleashed an untamed beast, but in truth Modern architecture was already a dried prune, its vitality long spent. What most Modernists were doing was called "the built diagram." Dry, predictable, and banal.

What de Botton and Venturi realized was that "buildings speak," an axiom that architects have either forgotten or not yet fully realized. To restore a universal language to architecture, the community needs to register the importance of the death of the author and the dangers in the myth of the creative genius. Architects, de Botton insisted, suffer under the terrible weight of having to invent forms that are ever new. We live in an age where developers and architects do not adhere to the rules and try to reinvent the wheel on every street corner.

It should be notions of comment by Robert Venturi and Alain de Botton that infiltrate the creative culture. A sense of stepping back from the vortex that is creation and seeing the rational, the needed and the resolutions – whilst maintaining a breadth of vision for the collective.

Kitchen sink realism, "A Taste of Honey," and The Smiths

Occurring in England just prior to Venturi, an English cultural movement could be seen in various creative media. Fuelled by the racial, class, and sexual tensions of a working class, England neighborhood-in-transition films had raw storylines, grittiness, political commentary, sardonic humor. They were always set in the North of England, the bastion of the industrial working class. It was a celebration of the everyday; about small things that gradually grew large; films that had politics that were oblique, humor that was unexpected, emotions that gained power though restraint. This newfound interest among young people also found painters using domestic scenes as subjects, with stress on the banality of life. Artists painted several kitchen subjects, often turning practical utensils such as sieves and spoons into semi-abstract shapes, and thus for art it was the introduction to social realism for the onlookers of the day. The colloquial terms were also notable in the films and novels of the time. Regional situations, accents, and themes made the films and theater accessible.

An example here is the 1958 play by British dramatist Shelagh Delaney, *A Taste of Honey*, which segues the innocence of earlier British cinema into more modern harsh realities. Also, a combination of a frankness about sex, and a more political content (sometimes descending to rants) led to a clean break with the assumptions of 1950 in the arts generally. *A Taste of Honey* confronts a range of social issues – single motherhood, race, sexuality – from a female point-of-view and with frankness, both unusual for the 1950s in Britain. The play and its film adaptation were influential in changing the public's attitude towards art and society. Set in Salford in Lancashire, the play tells the story of Jo, a 17-year-old working class girl whose mother, a crude, sexually indiscriminate "slapper," abandons her after finding a rich and considerably younger lover. She finds a room with Geoffrey, a gay acquaintance, and becomes pregnant after sleeping with Jimmy, a black sailor. Geoffrey assumes the role of father until Jo's mother returns, when the future of her new family is put into question. Some 24 years later, in 1982, at a time when the fossils of Britain's punk scene were eroding at the birth of the synthesized New-Wave phenomenon, a creative partnership began in Manchester that would last a mere five years and yet alter the arc of British POP music. Between 1982 and 1987, The Smiths, fronted by an icon known only by his last name, *Morrissey*, stirred several outbursts of outrage from Britain's self-appointed moral guardians, and scenes of fan hysteria on a scale not seen since the heyday of glam rock a decade previously. Perhaps more importantly, though, The Smiths were able to merge highbrow and lowbrow influences, which soon became a Morrissey signature of sorts. The quintessential Morrissey line, "I dreamt about you last night and I fell out of bed twice," turns out to be lifted, word for word, from Shelagh Delaney's great kitchen sink drama, *A Taste of Honey*. It is perhaps the single most quoted source in the Smiths' canon. "Hand in Glove," "This Charming Man," and "This Night Has Opened My Eyes," all borrow from Salford-born Delaney's seminal drama of northern working-class life.

The Smiths were manna from heaven for bedroom adolescents, for whom Morrissey was nothing less than a mirror – and a vindication – of their thwarted dreams and desires. His hybrid aesthetic is part high camp, part English eccentric, part POP-cultural pick and mix, part Mancunian drollery. They elevated a certain kind of poetic provincialism to a POP art form and inadvertently crossed both the paradigms of POP. They, as artists, were articulating a notion of inward reflection as an outward critique (to the most susceptible of audiences). On the other side of their production was the record label, only interested in the commercial viability and financial success of the group. Creatively and lucratively The Smiths had a dark side, though, and that too was somehow quintessentially English. Morrissey sings of England, of something black, absurd, and hateful. The sense of possibility that their best songs contain is the possibility that a "simple" POP song could be as potent and as intimate, as literate and as allusive, as any other kind of great writing.

Duane Hanson

Pushing this species of POP realism was American-born artist Duane Hanson, who spent his life's work creating super-realist sculptures cast from human models. Hanson also describes the everyday, the masses, their starkness and intricacies, with deeply sorrowful humor. What is interesting about his work is the banality of each sculpture, the ordinariness and the honesty. And it is this very reason which makes them so compelling. They are mostly overweight, unattractive, dirty and their expressions are blank and lifeless. The recipe for his blatant critique of 1960–70s America was to pluck these "people" from their daily lives and to make a direct replication of them in the stark, sterile spatiality of a gallery. It meant the sculptures, in all their artificial perfection and lifelikeness brought forth bewilderment, astonishment, and dismay in all viewers. The American POP artists of the '60s, who produced usually direct, literal renderings of commonplace objects, such as soup cans and Brillo boxes, undoubtedly encouraged Duane Hanson to yield to his naturalistic inclinations. One of the first sculptures Hanson created after moving to South Florida in 1965 was *Abortion*, a two-foot-long mixed-media rendering of a dead pregnant woman sprawled on a table and covered with a sheet. *Abortion* reveals that by 1965 Hanson had not only embraced realism unabashedly, but that he had begun to comment on contemporary life.

> *I'm not duplicating life. I'm making a statement about human values.*
> [Duane Hanson]

Viewers and readers who dare to move in close are rewarded with details that could never be studied so candidly in real life: wrinkles, facial hair, fingernail dirt, and imperfections. And yet Hanson's objective was never blatant voyeurism, but the opening of a view onto those things we prefer to overlook: to the dullness of everyday life, and the ever-present intimation of mortality.

Hanson was a social realist, looking at a range of people in society and making observations about their condition in life. He recognized and admired ordinary people, like laborers and the elderly, whom he believed had been marginalized by society. Through his art he sought to make the public aware of their presence and contributions to society.

below and right
Battersea, London, 2006
JoAnn Kneedler

JoAnn Kneedler

Fast forward twenty years, and the human condition is again called forth as a portal to reflect by Brighton-based photographer JoAnn Kneedler. Her investigations begin with the question of control, coverage and human-movement manipulation. The work is critical of the systems of signage that she has encountered in her own movement around her environment. Her photographs act as a lens through which the public can reassess their urban condition. This series portrays the use of signage in London and Brighton – it alerts us to the incessant over-information, and exposes the modern society of constriction and "unprivacy" in which we live. Contemporary photographers easily nest themselves in work that demands merely commercial-based ventures. Advertising and the consumerist culture begin to become a field in which the modern photograph is bound. The other, more critical stream, the stream Kneedler has chosen to adopt, allows her to remove us from the day-to-day cycles that structure our movements. Kneedler's role is particularly poignant, as her work comes at a highly vexed time for a resident of London. A subsequent running theme is safety. Thereafter, contained within her work are threads of issues pertaining to greater needs for human control. With recent terrorist attacks, the advent of hosting the 2012 Olympic Games, and the infamously dangerous urban condition have brewed this capitalist control of the streets. It is only within the removal of oneself from such a condition, or the physicality of the photograph, that allows one to fully comprehend it. Kneedler is saving us. Helping us realize the magnitude of this "dominative" condition allows us to be critical of our government and physical environment. The method in the way we move now has a further understanding, and perhaps allows us to be more aware and confident.

Ari Versluis and Ellie Uyttenbroek

As a photographic comparison, Rotterdam-based Ari Versluis and Ellie Uyttenbroek also take the "city as context that defines us" as subject and share an interest in making aware the striking similarities between various social groups. The "research" is formed as a systematic document of numerous identities.

"Exactitudes" 82. French Touch – Bordeaux 2006
Ari Versluis and Ellie Uyttenbroek

Exactitudes – in this case a contraction of the terms "exact" and "attitude." By registering their subjects in an identical framework, with comparable poses and a strictly observed physical code (a catalog), Versluis and Uyttenbroek provide an almost scientific, anthropological record of people's attempts to distinguish themselves from others by assuming a group identity. Using the repertory of the street to the studio backdrop, the series offers a purposely absurd response to the sentimentality of the beloved spontaneity of the photo booth.

What results is a selection of groups of people who looked exactly the same as each other. Their research has identified some "groups" including leathermen, massalas, grannies, and game boys. The members of the sub-cultural groups are fittingly selected so that they are consistent with the catalog and also represent the wanting of the subjects. The artists have ironically realized that most of the participants are unaware that they possess any similar traits to their "style-siblings." "When you show them polaroids of the others from that group they sometime say, why do you want to take my picture, you already have one? ... especially with the old people." *Exactitudes* can therefore be regarded as a sociological study of a multicultural society. It is actively allowing our generation to step back and see the peculiar and homogeneous way in which we exist. Somewhat like a macro study of a micro-organized society that captures the spirit of an era.

William Blake's "Milton: a Poem"

Between the years 1804 and 1810, "far and away the greatest artist Britain has ever produced," William Blake penned an ode to a fellow poet. *Milton: a Poem* is about John Milton, who gallantly returns from Heaven and unites with Blake. The verse discusses the relationship between their poetic peers and the writers who came before them – it speaks of the progress toward the apocalyptic union of the living and the dead, internal and external reality, male and female, human and non-human.

And did those feet in ancient time
Walk upon England's mountains green?
And was the holy Lamb of God
On England's pleasant pastures seen?

And did the Countenance Divine
Shine forth upon our clouded hills?
And was Jerusalem builded here
Among these dark satanic mills?

Bring me my bow of burning gold;
Bring me my arrows of desire;
Bring me my spear; O clouds, unfold!
Bring me my chariot of fire!

I will not cease from mental fight,
Nor shall my sword sleep in my hand,
Till we have built Jerusalem
In England's green and pleasant land.
[William Blake]

In one of Blake's two final epics, Milton follows the hero in a journey of self-discovery and renewal. In the poem's first "Book," John Milton returns from Heaven to the mortal world and unites with the imagination through the person of William Blake. Together, they set out to re-configure the relationship between a living poet and a great predecessor. The work was written to give the author the opportunity to say something that he wouldn't have otherwise had a chance to say. Instead of treating Milton like anyone who had been dead for more than a hundred years, the treatment of Milton's thought also supposes that it exists through an "Emanation, Sixfold presumably because he had three wives and three daughters." In fact, after John Milton had become blind, his wives and daughters represented a tremendous portion of his remaining contact with the world.

The giving up of self-hood that Blake allows in Milton is to achieve a more inclusive sense of self – essential for the artist to create. Blake assumed a society in which people were actually being taught things like a Platonic belief in forms. And the Classics were a large element of what seemed bad to him. He might have felt differently if he ever had a chance to observe our formless void, where any claim to wisdom is highly suspect. The vying for a human portrayal as one that morphs Milton is a choice to ground a seemingly unreachable, ethereal character in Blake's mind. For reasons similar to the intentions of the Bible, one can draw a parallel to Christ as the figure of a man among us which reveals an accessibility of a transcended figure. For the pleasure of Blake, his readers, and the eternal Milton, we read his predecessor as real, unabridged yet omnipotent through prose – a humbling gesture.

Caravaggio and "Young Sick Bacchus"

At a time when it was believed artists were given their talent by God – to bring beauty to the world and to put mortal creatures in touch with their higher selves, their souls – Michelangelo Caravaggio was experimenting with a type of art that delivered truth. "What begins in the work of Caravaggio is, quite simply, modern painting." However, he was often cast as the black sheep of Italian Baroque painting, as he employed a theatrical realism and sacrilegious subject matter that infuriated critics of the time. Subsequently, it forced him into obscurity, and continues to raise eyebrows even today. The arresting painting of a young, flushed Bacchus – a self-portrait done during convalescence from a serious illness – is one of his most famous. Dated between 1593 and 1594, the livid colors of the subject's face, his teasing smile and the mock seriousness of his mythological dignity all reinforce the attempt to undermine the lofty pretensions of Renaissance artistic traditions. Here is no God, just a sickly man who may be suffering from the after-effects of a hangover. There is no mistaking the artist's delight in the depiction of the fine peaches and black grapes on the slab, the white grapes in his hand and the vine leaves that crown his hair. But the artist is not content merely to demonstrate his superb technique: He wishes to play an intimate role, and only the slab separates him from the viewer. His appearance is striking rather than handsome; he shows both that his face is unhealthy and that his right shoulder is not that of a bronzed Adonis, as convention required, but pale as in the case of any man who normally wears clothes.

Caravaggio, like Blake, wishes to blur the esoteric. Both attempt to "de-spiritualize" the widely adopted perception of their subjects. A process that brings a sense of attainability in the layman's pursuit of a confrontation with their God, be it in any or many forms.

On a POP approach in architecture

Having discussed this series of works it becomes obvious that it is hard to be profound about architecture when there are problems within its contemporary state on the international stage. Only "sensitive" architects can see these problems – not developers, not the general public, and not other architects. The fundamental problem is that architecture often can be whittled down to the "image." Gone are the times when architecture was considered the highest form of art, and society would gasp at every pen-stroke that the architect so responsibly scribed. What is actually happening now is that a handful of infinitely well-connected firms are running the entire industry, they employ cheap, skilful people (most of the time not even architects) to produce iconic images that will, in turn, continue to win them competitions and keep the balance ticking over. Time and time again the same images keep coming up, lacking any real substance in their response to a brief.

Transplantation
The *Arbeitsamt* is placed into a housing system, more human in scale, and functions there unequivocally.

Concentration should therefore not be on the idols within the process of creation, but on those creators who take the issues of the time, the complexities of a decision, the facets of the program, and begin to dissect, mutate, scramble, and justify. POP is successful in that from the outset it is very appealing, it captures the essence of what is being sold to you. As with the world of consumerism, the "image" shows you something you want. But in the old laborious fight between needs and wants the same adage applies; POP should be looked at in relation to what people are in need of, not from the position of what they desire.

Three points govern the formulation parameters, in no particular order, 1: *A Needed Program*, 2: A considerable *Natural Population*, and 3: A Portion of *Silicon*. Drawing up a thought-out list and trying to find a program or scheme that not only follows these parameters but also challenges it, my suggestion was to design an *Arbeitsamt* – an unemployment office. This program then allows me to tackle real issues, to ground the function in the tribulations of mankind, and to formulate a resolution aligned to those who I am referencing.

Aiming to design a POP building, the focus was not on understanding POP architecture as a fad or a trend in time, but rather I wanted to consider POP architecture in terms of something being popular by numbers.

POP is about the real people

Having established the interest in something popular by numbers, the defining of architecture had reached its first plateau. The building should accommodate a program that required a large amount of visitors. The second and most obvious factor that makes a piece of architecture numerically popular is the amount of people required to use it (*A Needed Program*). Specifically this could relate to site and location within a city. It could also depend on the population of the city in which it is situated (*Natural Population*). Thirdly, with considerably less emphasis, and more with the understanding that it is superficial, is the admittance that aesthetics are also a factor in making a building POP (*Silicon*). I wouldn't like to spend any more time explaining this factor, as it has horrible odds in the "truly successful architecture" stakes.

Facts

1: Berlin has a 22% unemployment rate, while the nation musters 9.7%. That means that there must be a lot of people using these buildings and determines them *A Needed Program*. 2: Berlin has 3.4 million inhabitants, which passes the test of achieving an adequate *Natural Population*. 3: Interestingly, this factor becomes ironically important as these buildings, both interiorly and exteriorly, need a dramatic face-lift. An injection of *Silicon*, call it what you will.

Upon a visit to an Arbeitsamt in Berlin, hidden beneath its neo-fascist facade, I found a space that, shared with 30 or so confused, depressed, out-of-work citizens of Berlin, serves only to fuel or assist the negative mental state of its hopefully temporary tenants. Going there allowed me to entrench myself in the culture and lifestyle of one of the 750,000 unemployed Berliners, to become familiar with the psyche of a resident. It helped me ask critical questions, like what sort of spatial phenomenon relates to these people and how do they want to feel in the space.

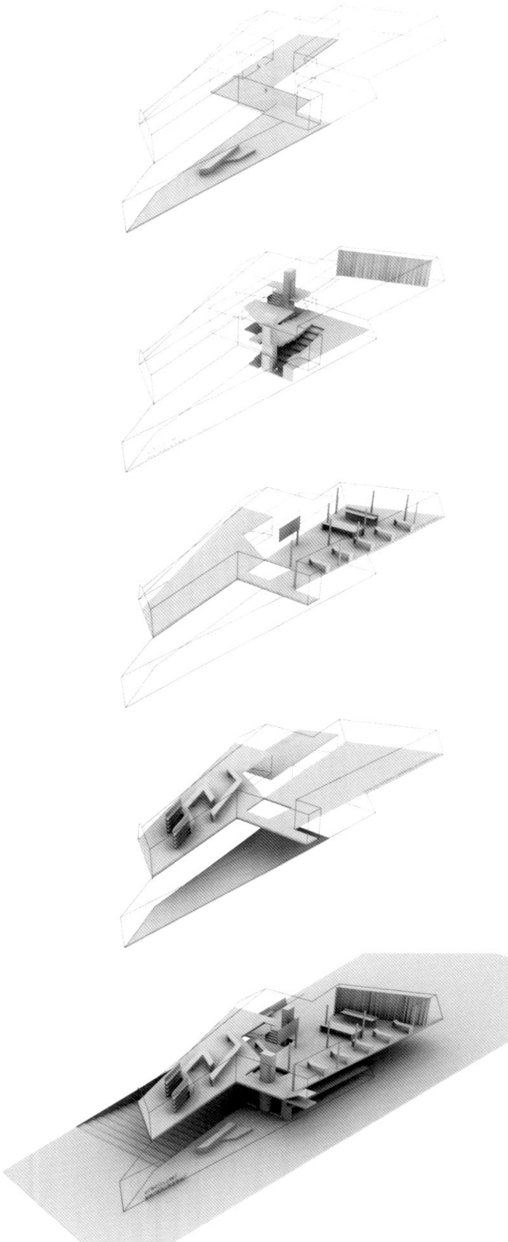

left
Exploded view
depicting the different spatial divisions of the *Arbeitsamt*

right
Exterior perspective

Gropius is a bosom

For a design with such a specific program and intention of phenomenon, my filtering brought me to the Bauhaus. The Bauhaus prided itself on its wide-ranging, cross-discipline approach, melding art with design. Marcel Breuer was an advocate of what has become a Bauhaus mantra, "Form follows function," claiming that if an object was designed in such a way that it fulfilled its function clearly, it was successful. The Bauhaus was active in Weimar, Dessau and Berlin, founded in 1919 by Walter Gropius, and closed down by the Nazi authorities in 1933. Aside from the more well-known contributions it gave, I found reference in the private work of Gropius and more poignantly his design for an Arbeitsamt in Dessau (1928–29). The Arbeitsamt is a two-storey administration block and a protruding one-storey circular building with a glazed shed roof for the public. Amongst all the programmatic decisions based on coping with the large numbers of visitors, (i.e., a ground plan that would permit the public to be channeled and separated according to sex and profession) the façade of the circular building was without windows, its interior gave cause for wonder thanks to the shed roof, which allowed light to flood into the building from above. The interior walls in the upper part of the building are made of glass, so that light can flood right through the building. The building was so radical in its approach, as its programmatic counterparts were (and still are, polemically) constructed with a gamut of non-humanist parameters that work against the possible subliminal/psychological benefits that design could bring to such a vexed and sensitive program.

nordbahnhof
arbeitsamt

The spaces are articulated with the intention of integrating the human. Gropius works with gestures such as reducing scale, the use of vernacular materials and the inclusion and generous distribution of light. In his article entitled *Architecture at Harvard University*, which first appeared in *Architectural Record* in May 1937, he talks about the intended contributions he wishes to make to the development of American architecture students, as the newly-appointed Head of the GSD at Harvard. "My intention is not to introduce a so-to-speak cut-and-dried 'Modern Style' from Europe, but rather to introduce a method of approach which allows one to tackle a problem according to its peculiar conditions. I want a young architect to be able to find his way in whatever circumstances; I want him independently to create true, genuine forms out of the technical, economic, and social conditions in which he finds himself instead of imposing a learned formula onto surroundings which may call for an entirely different solution." This intention suggested an open, flexible development for his students and evidently for the occupants of his Arbeitsamt in Dessau. These same intentions were translated into the floors, walls, and roofs of his intrinsic, manifold architecture. And he continues, voicing an opinion relevant to today: "More than ever before is it in the hands of us architects to help our contemporaries to lead a natural and sensible life instead of paying a heavy tribute to the false Gods of make-believe. Good architecture should be a projection of life itself and that implies an intimate knowledge of biological, social, technical, and artistic problems."

The continuum of his ideology was seen again in 1956, commenting on the average human being. He stated that one "will feel the need for a more beautiful and more organically coherent environment as an expression of his pride and participation in our democracy, then he may cause a chain reaction conducive to solving our great and complicated task, to have both, unity and diversity, the two indispensable components of a cultural order."

The architecture

The humble scale of Gropius' Arbeitsamt transforms the idea of an unemployment office into a human experience, complete with familiar materials and a sensitive control of light. The same was applied to my proposal for the *Arbeitsamt* in Berlin.

Gropius' Arbeitsamt and indeed my design take the approach of "domestifying" the inhumanely scaled.

A tactic of doing this is the inclusion of brick in the building's material set. Brick is a memorable material normally defining living quarters. For this reason, the *Arbeitsamt* is cloaked in a memorable space, accessible with features of one's own experience and living. This phenomenon is amplified further by the control of light, the definition of programmed spaces and framed views. A mixture of these intentions aspires to create something accessible and human.

Conclusion

The *phalanstères* outlined in this text deal with the thoughts administered by the people. All of the creators' work is routed in the considered, calculated and personal, and have benefited the sociological and environmental realms. They are productions that reflect on the human condition. Whether it is Venturi's Modernists criticisms, de Botton's quest for beautiful architecture, The Smiths' capturing of human emotion, Kneedler's reflection of the human condition, Versluis & Uyttenbroek's cataloging of types, Blake's reincarnation of his fellow poet, Caravaggio's God-as-Man ideology, or Gropius' humanizing of the Arbeitsamt, the aim is to engage in blatant re-assessment in order to access those things we prefer to overlook, to see the conditions of everyday life and our own final mortality. There is a collective hope for a realization, through their art, that they can open the eyes of the masses, to step back and observe humanity – and architecture, through its process and execution, is attempting to do the same thing.

Section and ground floor plan
Main entrance, lobby, circulation, and office spaces

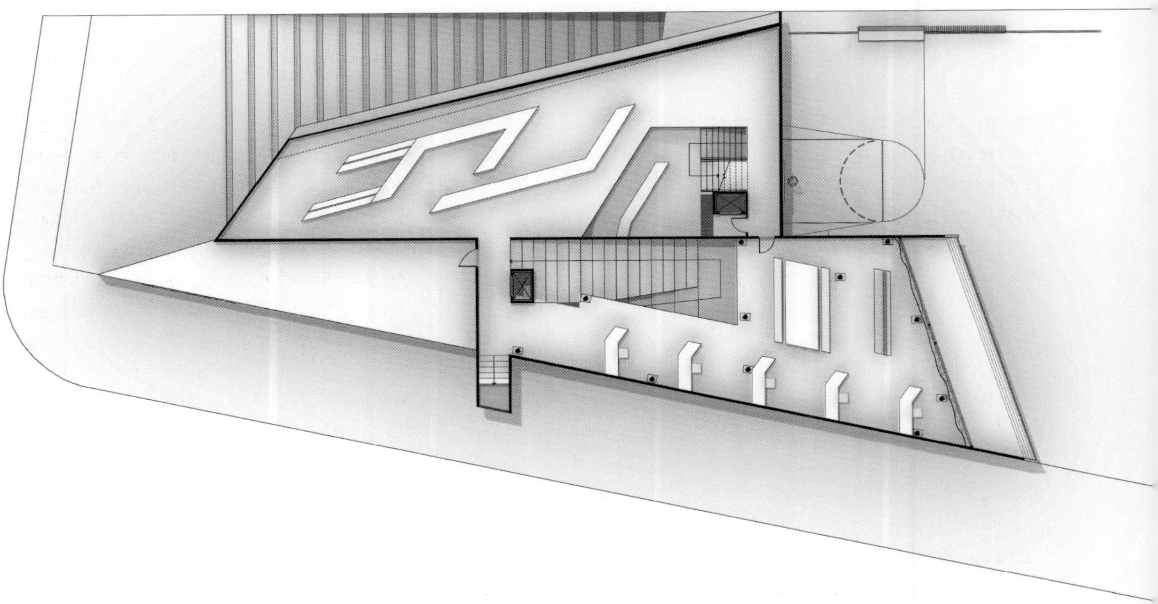

SELECTED – THE NEW EXPERIENCE OF CONSUMPTION

Kalina Aleksandrova, Julie Hoffmann

Selected is not a supermarket, it's a brand. It stands for high-quality, ecological nutrition, which has become increasingly popular in recent years. To give people an adequate environment for shopping their desired organic products we have derived the concept for our *Selected* building from an organic structure, the cell. Using the element of the cell allows us to produce the image of an organic whole – the building and its products. As the architecture of *Selected* underlines and supports our consumers' quest for quality, biologically-friendly products, it becomes itself part of the cultural phenomenon POP.

POP philosophy

Adieu, Birkenstock-Sandals! Organic foods get a long-overdue make-over! For years, many people associated dried-up carrots and canvas shopping bags with organic food stores. Most avoided such shops because they were considered more expensive and more weird than regular supermarkets. In fact, numerous people even derided organic food lovers, who bought their tofu and muesli in health food stores. Today, the target group of those interested in organic foods is enormous. However, though the modern person is becoming progressively more health conscious and demanding, today's market has not risen to satisfy their demands.

Like POP music allowing people to indulge in emotions, the POP architecture of our building allows the consumer to indulge in the world of an organic whole – the building and its products.

As the consumer and eating culture of people has changed, nutrition has evolved from a mere necessity to a central and integral part of life in modern society. Even the mass media have reacted accordingly. The hype doesn't stop at products themselves; instead, it has been taken to a higher and more POP level as shopping and cooking shows on "prime time" television depict young, attractive people showing us how to cook, where to shop, how to eat, and where to buy the dinner wear – basically how to live a more organic, healthy, and chic life. These impulses for healthy perfection and popularity have led to an insane obsession with food. Yet no organic food supermarket has arrived which fully answers the needs of these customers. Thus our goal is to provide organic food lovers with an environment that responds to their basic needs – organically grown nutrition.

Our interest in POP architecture was to take the popularization of organic food into the building and utilize it as the fundamental mechanism for selling products. Therefore the *Selected* building is organized and works like an organic structure, implementing the cell, the smallest structural and functional unit of an organism, as its basic space module.

The supermarket as we know it ...

with endless rows of overcrowded shelves ...

and long lines at the cash registers

The *Selected* experience ...

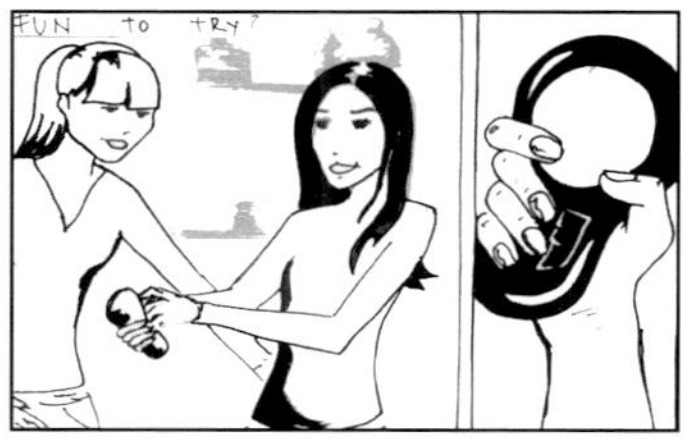

pictures shopping as pleasurable ...

in a suitable environment

The concept of the Selected building

The biological plant cell is the iconic as well as structural and functional image of the overall concept of the *Selected* building. This shopping concept seeks to provide a series of lounges, each devoted to a different product. Here, the costumers are invited to look at, touch, and test the displayed sample products. They then order the chosen item from the storage rooms and pick it up on their way out.

The architecture of all rooms is based on modular cell-like spaces. The outer façade and the interior walls are a layer of rigid, semi-transparent membranes. The walls serve as structural elements and as a transport system for all products. When you order, your items travel through the mechanical walls to the exit where you will purchase them. As the envelope of this transport system is semi-transparent, the constant movement of the product silhouettes becomes a specific visual experience. Inside the cell-like spaces there are special installations, so-called digital trees, displaying the available product. Next to the pure iconography derived from the plant cell, the customers are offered a theme-park-like experience that turns shopping into a non-stressful and memorable event. Answering the economical needs of a firm, all installations are non-permanent and allow the flexibility to quickly adapt to new developments in the market.

The essence of POP architecture is not to erect buildings the "cheap and fast" way. Rather, it is a systematic approach towards the design and production of new, contemporary spaces and atmospheres. The *Selected* building is an elaborate and technologically refined structure, flexible enough to grow and expand – but definitely always linked to its goal of providing the modern and fashionable organic food consumers with a building that will offer them the perfect, *Selected* shopping experience.

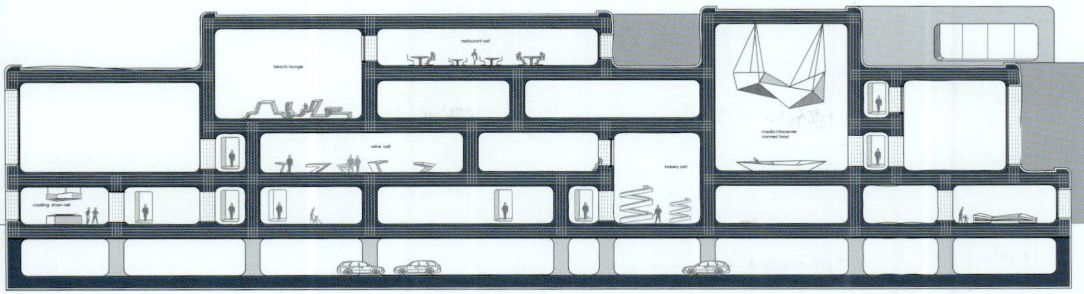

above

Section through the building

explaining the structure of the cells for shopping and relaxation

below

Main entrance and urban plaza

3 POP(ULARITY)

COME PLAY WITH ME – IN SEARCH OF POP(ULARITY)

Riklef Rambow – in conversation with Daniela Konrad and Jason Danziger

PEP – POP EDUCATION PALACE

Anna von Roeder, Berta Sola Sánchez

SUPERPLAY VIDEO GAME CENTER

Andreas Bengtsson

COME PLAY WITH ME – IN SEARCH OF POP(ULARITY)

Riklef Rambow – in conversation with Daniela Konrad and Jason Danziger

Riklef Rambow talks about his definition of the cultural phenomenon POP – linked to sex, drugs, and rock and roll, youth and stardom. Referring to POP art and POP music he lifts the lid on a series of characteristics of POP and their uneasy relationship to architecture.

RR Riklef Rambow
DK Daniela Konrad
JD Jason Danziger

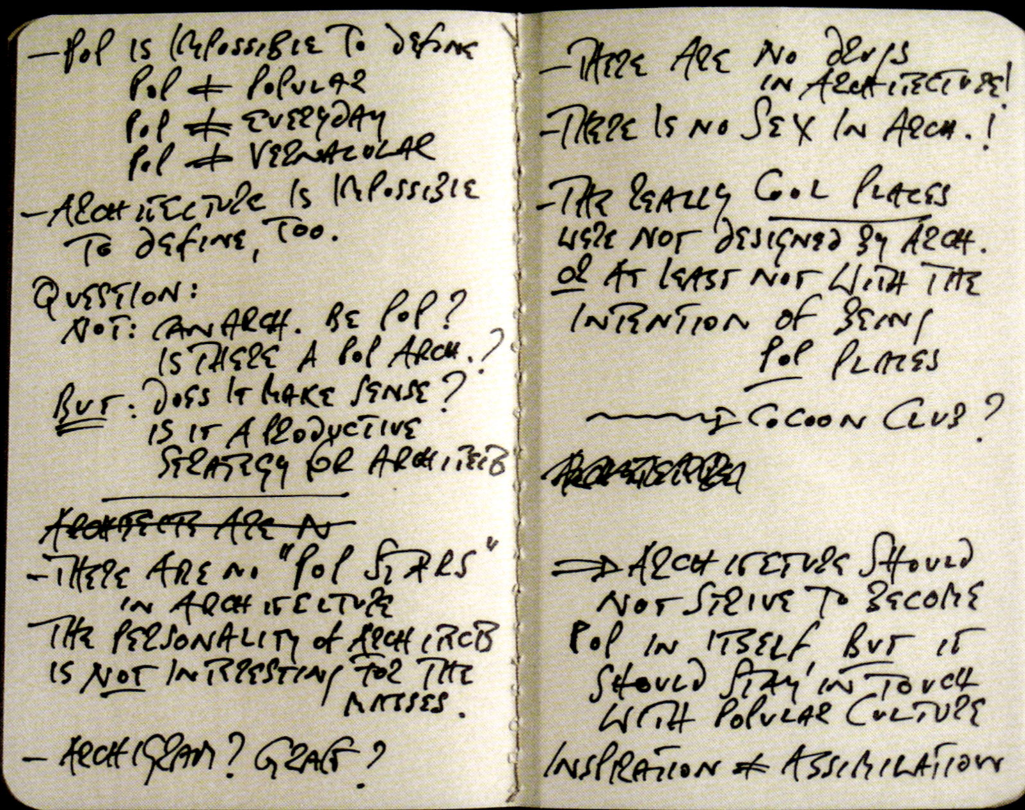

DK. Riklef, we want to talk about the ideas that you shared with us during your lecture at our symposium on POP architecture. You mentioned that POP has a strong relationship with sex and drugs, and that the cultural phenomenon POP produces and, in turn, is dependent on POP stars. But according to you there are neither sex, drugs nor POP stars in architecture, hardly anybody cares about the private lives of architects, and people do not display posters of architects on their walls. I wonder if we should dispense with the traditional definition of POP and admit that architecture nowadays is trying to produce icons and signs as representations of wealth and power; for example, oversized and "over-designed" houses which are more like spectacles than functional homes. Isn't it feasible that architecture could include POP aspects or even be POP?

RR. When I tried to define the term POP at the symposium, I deliberately started from a provocative point of view, saying that POP should have to do with sex, drugs, and rock and roll, which, in my eyes, is sort of a classical definition of POP culture. Additionally, the cult of the POP star is a crucial component of POP. Searching for these elements in architecture, we have to admit that architecture at the moment is not very sexy, and also architects as persons are not very sexy, generally speaking. The majority of the people wouldn't go and buy a poster of, let's say, Frank Gehry. He is definitely considered to be a POP star in the architecture scene, but I would not describe him as a POP star per se.

Furthermore, the average age of architects who build is much higher than the age of POP stars in music. And that is a problem, if you are 40 years or older and just beginning to be a famous architect, you are too old to become a POP star for the teenager generation. I want to hold on to the idea that POP culture is an important way for the younger generation to express itself in a non-predetermined way. POP culture needs to provide opportunities for subversive actions and allow for a sort of an emotional acting out. You have to admit that this is a difficult task for architecture to fulfill. Besides, not only the age of the architect but also the fact that the process of producing architecture is expensive and takes a long time plays an important role. In fact, architecture is very knowledge-intensive, meaning you really need professional education to be able to construct buildings at all. Looking at music or art, everybody can easily point out several examples of POP stars who just joined the scene and were not professionals in their fields.

So, while in other disciplines one is able to just jump in, in architecture it is not feasible to just design and build some flashy, popular building.

I do not want to deny that there are certain buildings with a potential to be POP architecture, like the Guggenheim Museum in Bilbao. Surely this building has become part of general POP culture: It is widely known, often used as the background for fashion photography and it was even chosen as a location for a James Bond movie. But what is crucial to me is that, even if the Guggenheim Museum becomes part of POP iconography, that does not mean it is POP in and of itself.

JD. Architecture is always lagging twenty years behind other forms of creative expression. Often, when something appears in art or music it takes at least twenty years to be reflected in architecture. Two examples are minimalist art of the '60s and the minimalist architecture of the '80s. What interests me is the relationship between POP itself and today's youth. I think POP can often enable the powers that be to structure, formulate, and control public opinion. Because those in power – the people driving the POP car – are not young themselves, they just want to influence young people. So how can you precisely define the relationship between POP and youth?

RR. According to your statement, I seem to be referring to an old-fashioned, naïve idea of POP. But I am not sure if it still makes sense to talk about POP if you refer to TV shows like "POPstars," organized by old, boring guys, produced and promoted by the media system, lacking any kind of subversive moment or potential. So if you say that today Dieter Bohlen, Rupert Murdoch or Hubert Burda are the real POP stars, than you can indeed deny any serious relationship between youth and POP. But, contrary to this position, I would hold on to the idea that our society still allows young people to express themselves through POP in certain niches. For example, techno music was started by young people and for a while worked as a POP movement in this emphatic sense, before it was absorbed by the music industry for "big business" purposes. In this sense subversive movements are still possible. And even provocation can be expressed to a certain degree. But let us return to architecture. I would like to add that here you can form a group and start undermining conventions as well. Archigram is an example for such an approach. The medium they chose for their designs was paper. So their ideas got distributed right away and didn't suffer from that long development and construction process.

In this sense, if we talk about designing and publishing ideas in a magazine, it is indeed possible to work directly with POP ideas in architecture.

But then again, Archigram's work is probably closer to art than to architecture. Once the group or their remaining members are actually producing a building, with the Kunsthaus in Graz by Peter Cook and Colin Fournier, almost 40 years have passed, and the building differs substantially from the visions formulated by Archigram in the first place.

DK. Mentioning Archigram, I would like to know if your definition of POP in architecture is linked to utopian ideas. Can the designs of the '60s by Archigram be described as POP architecture?

RR. Maybe POP does not have to do with utopian ideas, but rather with irrational or counter-rational ideas: ideas boiling with energy that do not necessarily make sense but are developed just for the sake of it. This phenomenon actually contradicts architecture. In architecture, producing a building that really does not make sense, a building that is purely flamboyant, an orgy, or a built folly, is ultimately a question of money. It might be helpful to think of Versailles or Neuschwanstein, which exemplify the rare combination of absolute power and visions of grandeur. Fortunately, there are not many people who have either enough money or the desire to actually make such buildings materialize.

JD. Can you be more precise? You said that POP is always fun. So can we assume that if architecture is fun, then it is POP? I mean, buildings like Versailles or Neuschwanstein are in my opinion fun, but they are, as you mentionec, relatively rare. Most of the architecture that is constructed needs to take more responsibility and provide homes for people or venues for social events.

RR. Yes, the fun aspect is only one possible way of approaching the POP phenomenon in architecture. But there is no general definition saying that if architecture is fun then it is POP, because POP is fun. POP is always about a combination of factors. There is not one pure and straightforward definition of POP. I want to emphasize that POP is definitely a fuzzy concept. I can easily agree on the fact that architecture has certain sensitivity towards POP culture or relationship with it. And iconographic architecture is representing a part of a POP movement. When architecture appears in movies and advertisements, the wider public can be affected by its emotional power. In this case, buildings might work as images for a popular lifestyle. That is one example of a relationship between POP and architecture, and it is possible to show that they in fact can profit from each other. But again, that does not mean that there is a POP architecture per se. Otherwise you would have to admit that Friedensreich Hundertwasser is the closest you ever get to a POP architect. He has produced buildings with flashy aspects like golden domes that many people understand emotionally. Picture calendars and posters of his work are mass produced, and these you may indeed find in the rooms of 14 year old suburban adolescents.

DK. That is a very important point in the discussion on POP in architecture that you are mentioning. Hundertwasser in fact is not a major reference for architects, and he is often criticized within the profession. But after the Modern Movement, the Bauhaus period and the minimalist and brutalist architecture, which didn't offer the general public the possibility of feeling comfortable or understood, I think we can detect a POP movement in architecture which has resulted in more popular buildings by avant-garde architects, meaning architects who are admired and respected within contemporary architectural circles. And as a matter of fact, these buildings are still offering opposition to Hundertwasser's direction. What seems crucial to me is that this new POP phenomenon has actually led to the fact that many architects want to jump on the POP bandwagon and produce iconographic buildings with mass appeal: buildings that replace the architecture by Friedensreich Hundertwasser and are able to influence professional architectural discourse. Today, the "form follows function" has been replaced by a discourse about "popular visualization."

In Barceloneta, Barcelona, Spain

RR. You have to differentiate between popularity and POP. I tried to highlight this aspect in the title of my lecture "Come Play with Me – in Search of POP(ularity)." The orientation of architects towards popularity, the wish to be loved by ordinary people, is related to populism, but not to POP.

JD. During your lecture you said that architecture does not produce strong emotions. You quoted Umberto Eco and said that architecture is mostly background for emotions but does not provoke them. I think we can agree that emotions do play a part in POP culture. Some architects and designers, like Philippe Starck or Steven Holl, have built their careers on creating highly charged emotional spaces. And, there is a long tradition in literature (i.e., Marcel Proust and W. G. Sebald) who use architecture as a direct metaphor for emotions and who actually forge emotional "spaces."

I would like to know your thoughts about the following quote from Sebald's book *Austerlitz* (2001): "Until the 17th century the priory of the order of the Saint Mary of Bethlehem stood on the site of the present main station concourse and the Great Eastern Hotel. It had been founded by a certain Simon Fits Mary in gratitude for his miraculous rescue (...). Whenever I was in the station, Austerlitz said, I kept almost obsessively trying to imagine through the ever changing mains of walls the location in that huge space of the rooms where the in-silent inmates where confined. And I often wondered whether the pain and suffering accumulated on this site over the centuries had ever really ebbed away, or whether they might not still, as I sometimes thought when I felt the cold breath of air on my forehead, be sensed as we passed through them on our way through the station hall and up and down the flights of steps."

RR. Sebald is definitely not POP. He rather represents the opposite of POP and stands firmly on the grounds of an intellectual high culture. His thinking about the relationship between built structure and emotion is highly refined and subtle, his language very artful and elaborated. The same goes for Marcel Proust and the story of the madeleine. There, just the smell of the madeleine, a small cake, helps to reveal an entire world. Proust is starting a story from a seemingly small sensual experience and develops it throughout thousands of pages. Sure, architecture plays a role here and it functions as a starting point for remembrances and emotions, but in the most elaborated and artificial way.

So I can agree that buildings are part of our memories and are able to activate emotions, but I would nevertheless insistently oppose the idea that architecture raises strong emotions in the same way that POP is raising emotions, meaning in a direct unfiltered way. If you are sixteen years old and you have fallen in love with a girl, and your love is not returned, and you are losing your faith in this world, you feel you have to do something! Maybe you sit down and write a poem, or you make a collage, or write a piece of music, or you go to a concert, or watch some video-clip on MTV. And then you discover that somebody exactly expresses these same feelings in a song, and this song becomes "your" song. You will always remember the girl you have been in love with when somebody is playing it. Something like this usually does not happen with a piece of architecture.

A madeleine

JD. It is interesting to understand the madeleine as a mechanism, which functions, as you said, because it recalls emotions from another place. It might be called an "emotional displacement mechanism." And I think that POP often operates using this kind of mechanism (your example of the teenager who has strong emotions finding solace in the POP song which helps him/her cope). True, I am not a psychologist, but I do think that the madeleine, as a mechanism, operates quite strongly in architecture, too. As an example we could look at the Holocaust Memorial by Richard Serra and Peter Eisenman. This monument operates in the same way as the madeleine: it can provoke an emotional response and clarify a certain approach to a very difficult episode in history.

RR. Yes, there obviously has been the idea to build a monument which raises certain emotions. The Holocaust Memorial has the problem that it is meant to generate specific emotions and at the same time it has to avoid the impression of being too didactic. You find this ambiguity throughout all of Peter Eisenman's statements and you find it at the site itself, because many people obviously use it as a place where they have fun, play hide and seek, or make interesting photographs. Many tourists have not the slightest clue what it is meant for. Hardly anyone seems to experience moments of alienation or loneliness.

Interestingly enough, the *Ort der Information*, the relatively small museum beneath the memorial that was added later to the design, seems to be much more effective than the memorial itself in terms of emotional power. Maybe it's a bit of an exaggeration, but after all, a photograph of the concentration camps or some original document or leftover behind glass is emotionally much stronger – and more precise – than this huge architectural object that costs millions of Euros. In an article called *Grenzen der Entgrenzung: Architektur, Musik, Drogen* my co-author and I try to show that the possibility that architecture alone can produce feelings of the transgression or dissolution of boundaries is severely limited. And it is precisely these feelings that are very important in POP culture.

Going back to the example of the teenager, he/she can experience these moments in a club by means of ecstatic dancing, intensive music, or the use of legal or illegal drugs. These strong effects that you might experience in a club you cannot produce with architecture. In fact, the best clubs are often spaces that are either not designed at all or not designed by architects. In my lecture I referred to the Cocoon Club in Frankfurt, a very elaborately designed techno club. It is a nice space, but you really don't need all the effort for the intended emotional effect.

Buildings, even if they strive to raise emotions, remain products of an intellectual and technical process that is much more subtle and restrained.

You can become ecstatic by dancing in a very simple, improvised, and undesigned environment. To summarize, I think architecture has surely lots of qualities, but the ability to produce those in-the-face emotions that POP culture is requiring, is not one of the most obvious among them.

DK. I want to raise the question of whether we need to put architecture into another category and discuss it on another level than music or art. To more precisely describe my point, I want to give an example: a piece of POP music, let's say a song by Madonna, might as well provoke a happy and ecstatic feeling as unhappy and mournful emotions. And the expression of both kinds of emotions is generally accepted in the world of music. But if a building provokes sad and plaintive emotions, for example schools in the United States that are built to be re-used as prisons, these kinds of buildings are neither considered elaborated architecture nor POP architecture.

Memorial to the Murdered Jews of Europe
Known as the Holocaust Memorial
Berlin, Germany
Architect: Peter Eisenman

RR. Seems to me that you are arguing for a redefinition of POP so that architecture might fit into it. For me, there are too many criteria in POP culture that do not apply to architecture. In addition to the ones mentioned before I also want to raise the issue that architecture does not only operate on a fun-level. If architecture becomes a joke, it ignores function and use. Then POP architecture would simply be bad architecture.

RR. You are right. So referring back to the madeleine mechanism, one could say that all spaces can provoke emotions and that everybody has personal memories in which buildings do play an important role. But these places or buildings are not necessarily architectural spaces and they most likely have neither been constructed with the intention to cause emotions in the first place, nor are they related to POP culture. They achieve relevance by means of personal experience and appropriation. Maybe your example of the schools in the United States could even be an argument for the case that architecture should not try to be POP, because it would be highly cynical if an architect designed a building that purposefully evoked melancholy and sadness.

Looking back at the period of Postmodernism, some architects have dealt with architecture in a funny way and only rarely has the fun lasted very long. And in this sense I oppose the idea of defining a new category within POP culture where architecture could be operating. Architecture should observe POP culture carefully but it should not strive to become POP.

JD. But the question of whether POP music and POP architecture do belong in the same category has not yet been answered. For example I think it is extremely difficult and perhaps unfair to directly compare architecture with drugs. Architecture does operate on different levels, it does not have the potential to work as precisely as drugs, it operates more slowly and it is not meant to be a tool for radical expression of the younger generation. But if we try to understand architecture as playing in a different league, don't we have to state that architecture can be POP?

DK. You have written your PhD thesis about expert-layman communication in architecture. POP is a cultural phenomenon that attracted masses of people in the '60s and linked people from high society to low-income groups. The fact that POP began to play a role in architectural designs, touches on precisely this topic. If department stores look like evening clothes or if museums function as symbols for revitalized cities, equally admired by architects and laymen, isn't that strong evidence that a fusion of high and subculture is on its way in the architectural world? Does POP lead architecture's way towards an easier communication between client and architect?

RR. That is an interesting point. The iconic building is more easily accessible to certain parts of the population and a building like Future Systems' Selfridges Store in Birmingham does work quite well as a glamorous example. This kind of architecture does in fact incorporate a moment of direct communication, more so than the abstract and knowledge-intensive modern buildings.

To formulate it more precisely, the criteria for evaluation of this kind of architecture are more comprehensible to the masses. But exactly this aspect is then in turn criticized as being populist among architectural experts. It does not refer to the traditional criteria developed in architectural history and theory. Therefore, iconic buildings might well be considered as a kind of architecture that transgresses the borders of the discipline and opens up possibilities of communication. The question of whether iconic architecture should be considered POP still remains.

DK. The medial presence of the Guggenheim Museum in Bilbao provides a reputation for architecture that is surely open to discussion, but what I am interested in is the fact that this constant name-dropping on the mass media level is changing the architectural market and opening up new possibilities for the architectural profession. Recently the ZDF broadcasted a report on Rem Koolhaas describing him as "an iconic figure in architecture" and an "XXL architect." I must admit, I took delight in listening to these words, because I think it is a new phenomenon that architects are described in such slogan-like terms.

JD. You put your finger on a crisis in architecture. In recent decades, architects went in one direction and everybody else in the other. Architects have only rarely attempted to approach or bridge that gap. Most of them seem quite far from daily reality. In your lecture, you also mentioned that many trendy places, like bars or clubs, are not designed by architects. But I think POP could possibly offer architecture a way back into society, to reconsider the profession of the architect as a service for society. Is POP actually creating a "Coup d'État?"

DK. And yet another question is whether POP culture could initiate a new architectural approach toward building tasks like single family houses. Architects often rejected projects for the masses as being too simple. The issue here should not be to discuss POP versus populism, but the feasible chance of POP culture subverting existing power structures and allowing everybody – including architects – to rethink.

RR. Places for the masses unfortunately often tend to exemplify bad architecture. There are not many role-models for young architects who want to become successful by building low-key projects and still be taken seriously in the architectural scene.

Possibly, a POP approach in architecture has some potential to bridge the expert-layman gap, but POP is just one possible strategy among others.

RR. I do also believe that there is a change occurring in the perception of architects and architecture. But even though there are more interviews with architects on TV, the majority of the architects, and even the "big names" as Norman Foster, Rem Koolhaas, Zaha Hadid or Frank Gehry are still only famous among architects or architectural critics. The fact that somebody has visited the Guggenheim Museum in Bilbao does not automatically mean that he or she is able to recall the name of the architect or develops an interest in her/his personality. Architecture at large is still an elitist profession, and you are probably right when you say that most architects are really far away from the daily reality of the average person. Too many architects seem to take the popular success of a building as an indicator for a lack of quality. Often that works like some sort of automatic reflex: If everybody understands it, than something must be wrong.

To conclude, architecture has the advantage that it does not and can not solely operate on a POP level. It has to satisfy many other needs, like functional and technical requirements, like the very basic idea of keeping the rain out. And these additional demands should not primarily be considered as an obstacle but as an essential element of architecture.

Guggenheim Museum in Bilbao
Spain
Architect: Frank Gehry

PEP – POP EDUCATION PALACE

Anna von Roeder, Berta Sola Sánchez

Amusement and relaxation offer the smoothest access to people's minds. We are determined to mix two, sometimes opposing, aspects of society – education and pleasure. We present *PEP – the POP Education Palace*. A center incorporating a brand that stands for the collection of independent and objective facts, high quality information delivered directly to your mind. *PEP* is the place where this mix of education and entertainment will be put into practice. And this combination cannot be purely functional. It needs to be a spatial one. *PEP* defines a sequence of spaces that will carry the visitor through a mental metamorphosis. And exactly at the spatial intersection of media consumption and enjoyment, architecture becomes POP.

NewspaperSolarium

InternetShopping

RadioWhirlpool

The POP in PEP

A tremendous amount of information is flooding the markets. While demands on acquiring knowledge become increasingly important in our society, a trend of rejection of traditional education and the consumption of random information presented in the public media can be detected. This phenomenon of contemporary over-consumption of mass media and the growing rejection of classic education leads, according to us, to an obvious conclusion – the merger of the two. And we want to use entertainment as the instrument to link them. Thus the *Pop Education Palace* is about spaces for the education of the masses, offering the transmission of knowledge in a recreational and joyous manner.

The most obvious POP aspect of our approach is a programmatic one. It is derived from today's over-attention to mass media.

Central to our concept is the fact that public media like newspapers, television, or radio are capable of reaching all levels of society. They offer information from various fields which often guide our daily lives. Therefore, our approach is to educate people by broadcasting and transporting knowledge in a fun manner, and we propose a building in which the consumption of information is an enjoyable and relaxing activity. Furthermore, the visual and sensual design of the spaces created is influenced by POP. Even though the building volume needs to be somewhat carefully implemented and works as a mediator, it also claims to act as a provocative statement. The space becomes a built ideology, leveraging its popularity and broad influence on the mass media to defeat its superficiality by its own means.

To us POP is a very democratic process. It underlies changes through the intervention of society as a whole by supporting or abandoning new images, stars, styles, and ideas. Popular ideas are defined by transparent and thus comprehensible developments. *PEP* uses this insight to lead visitors through its intellectual and real space. It becomes a place, public and private, communicative and intimate at the same time. A place where people can go to see, meet, and learn in a way that in today's lifestyle comes naturally. But at the same time what people want to learn becomes part of this democratic process.

Educational buildings nowadays are often out of date and answer neither the functional nor the esthetical needs of our society. But education is an essential element that allows us to transport our knowledge across the ages. Thus, the appropriate space for future eduction is the *Pop Education Palace*. It offers high and low class people the opportunity to gather information and reflect on it in a leisurely environment.

Inspiration: Cedric Price's Fun Palace

The *Fun Palace* by Cedric Price was a project that presented spaces which offered unknown freedom in function and use to the anti-hierarchical and fun-oriented society in the 1960s. In fact, the fundamental changes from a manufacturing society to a knowledge-based economy generated a series of sweeping architectural proposals at that time. Cedric Price's *Fun Palace* was supposed to be a specific answer to the human needs of the time. It was designed to allow people to enjoy their life in spaces that offer a wide selection of entertainment facilities and almost endless options for the reshuffling of components according to its users' desires. To be able to fulfill the required leisure factor, the *Fun Palace* was supposed to span a considerable area and needed to be accessible from many points in the city. Furthermore it needed to be a regional and even national attraction, a place for political parties, cultural events, public discussions – a traditional forum, so to speak.

> *The subversive character of Cedric Price's Fun Palace has inspired us to design the POP Education Palace, yet PEP tries to specifically address the contemporary education mainstream. With the POP Education Palace we are radically aiming at mass approval by today's leisure society.*

Just as the *Fun Palace* references the social and cultural situation of its time, the *POP Education Palace* wants to take its conceptual strength from the idea of subverting current power structures (i.e., the mass media) as well as current social phenomena (i.e., the rejection of classic education). The *POP Education Palace* wants to offer specific spaces for information and education.

The programmatic fun-part of *PEP* is linked to the idea of Cedric Price as well, as *PEP* advertises different activities for different users. But while Price's machine-mega-structure offers "toolkits" to fit any sort of event in physical spaces, *PEP* offers tools to develop rather experimental "mental" spaces. Thus, Price's ephemeral and transformable space has been replaced by a static space that will allow change according to the media broadcasting information.

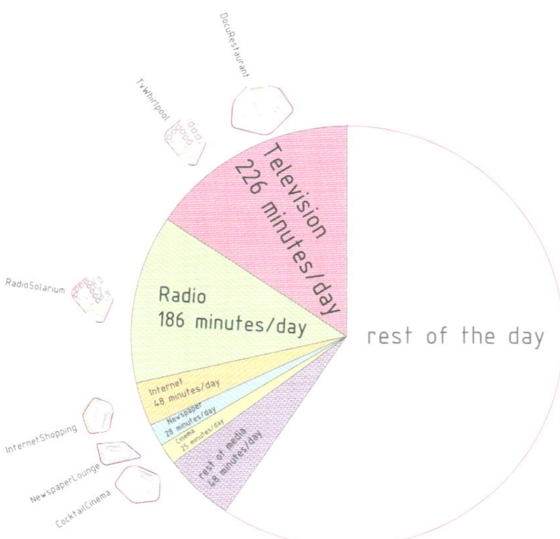

Space and size analysis
Use of different media within 24h

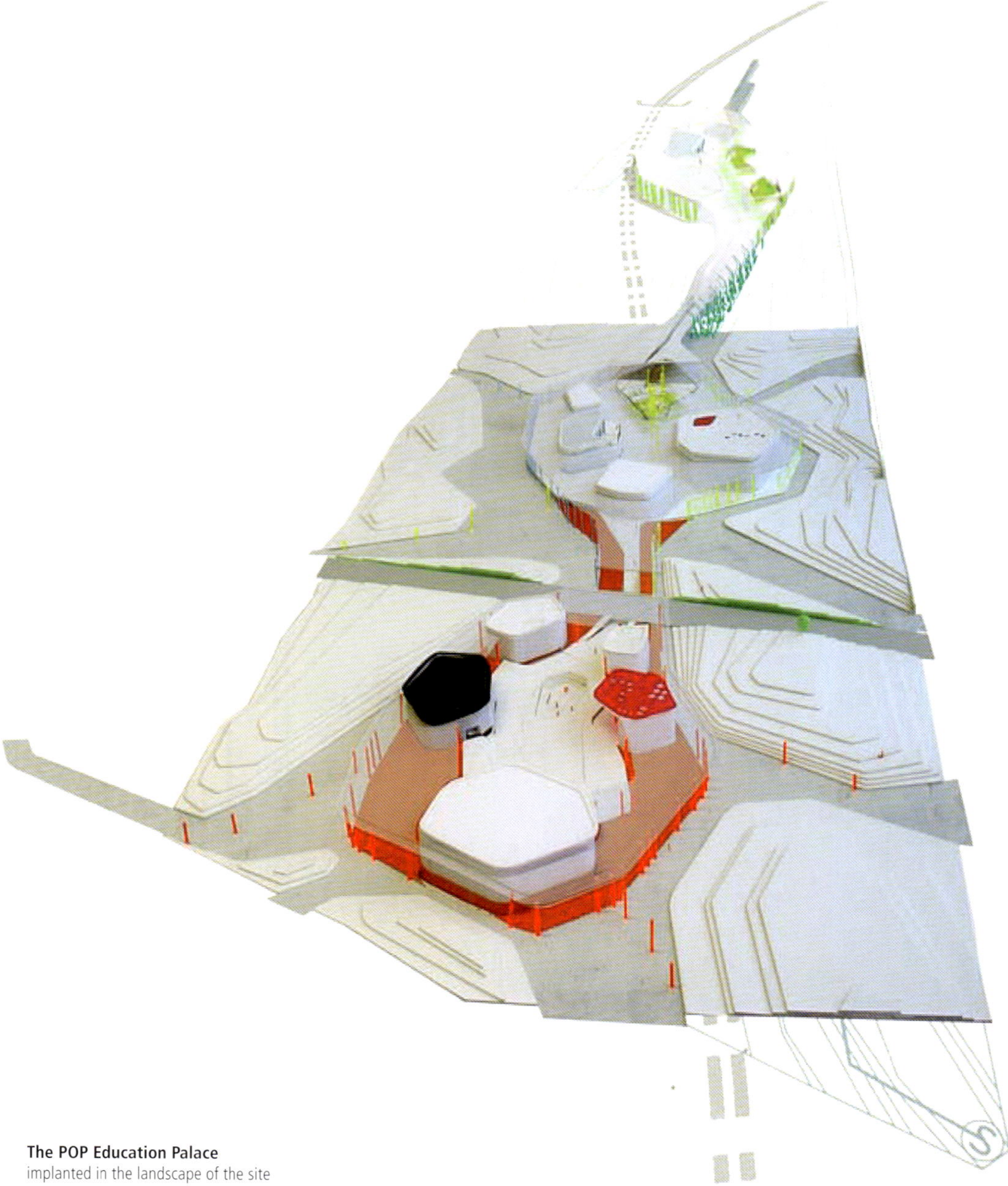

The POP Education Palace
implanted in the landscape of the site

The programmatic path

The programmatic path inside the *POP Education Palace* is founded on different activities of media consumption people pursue throughout a day. The inherent differences between possible day and night activities are projected on the program. Additionally, as mentioned, we created zones within the building that metamorphose from communicative via semi-public to private – areas which are subdivided into several "points of attraction." The path begins at the southern end of the plot where urban activities are most dense. Here is the main access point, and the generous plaza connecting the *POP Education Palace* to the city. This first stretch of the path is open to the public and supports communication and exchange. Towards the north of the project the layers of "quality-information" and entertainment become more intimate and personal. Wellness-facilities allow relaxation and the consumption of information at the same time. In the end the path becomes silent and almost meditative, staging a final and sensational view of the city.

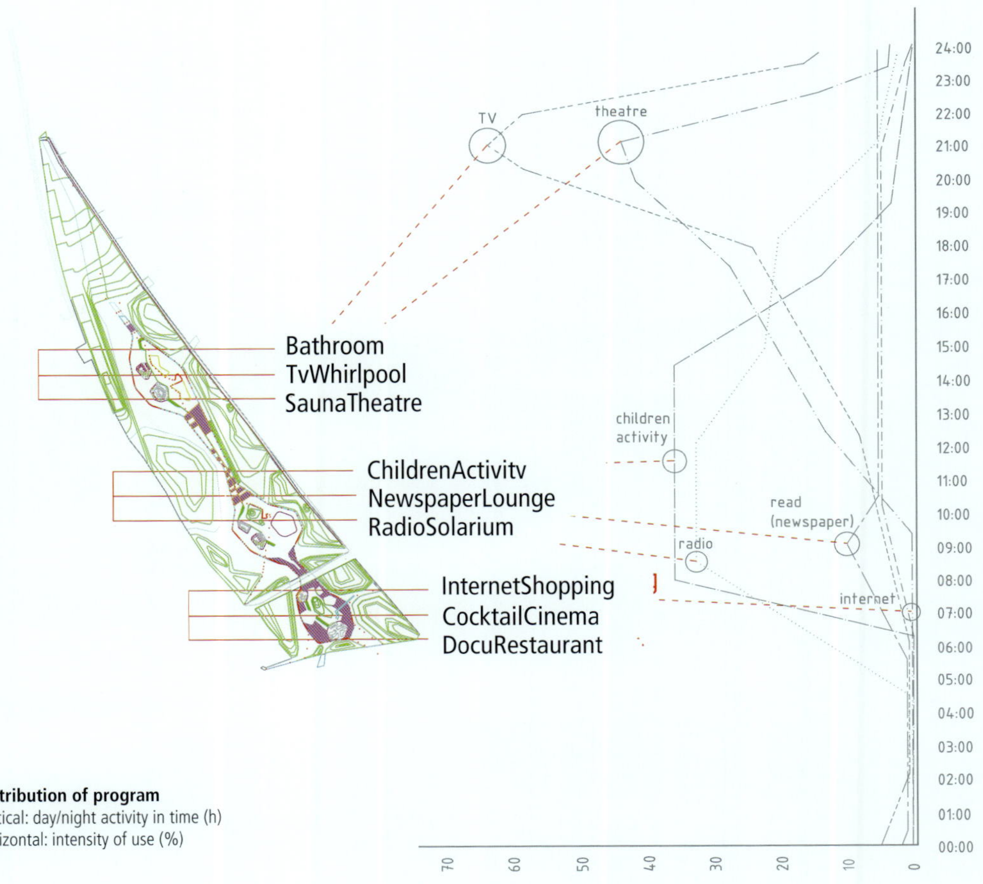

Distribution of program
Vertical: day/night activity in time (h)
Horizontal: intensity of use (%)

The inner organization

The different zones of the building are composed of several "stations." Each programmatic element is introduced in a "station," which is itself divided into two levels. On the lower level is the educational media space and on the upper level is the entertainment. They are always connected by the constant flow of information and by visual contact between the workers, who collect the information, and the visitors, who select and consume the information offered. The interior space of the *POP Education Palace* generates different ambiences and atmospheres, first more open and exteriorly orientated, and then slowly losing the direct connection to the ground, as if existing in an independent bubble. The light columns are an instrument to firstly guide the visitor, and secondly, to create a lucent atmosphere of relaxation and information flow at the same time. Features like the *Oasis* and the *Meditation Path* give the different atmospheres their identity.

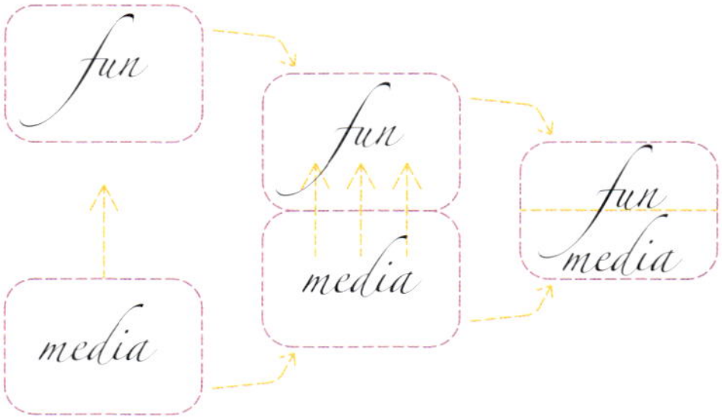

right
Atmosphere of the plaza

below
Connection between two "stations"

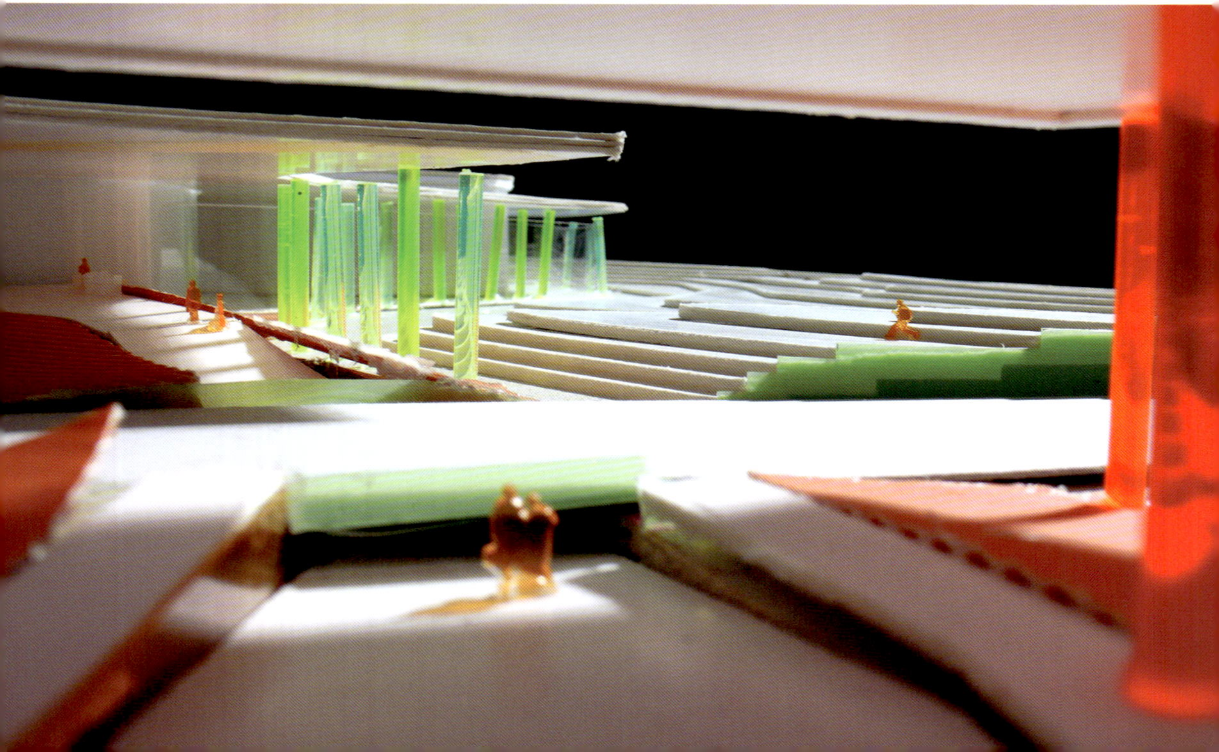

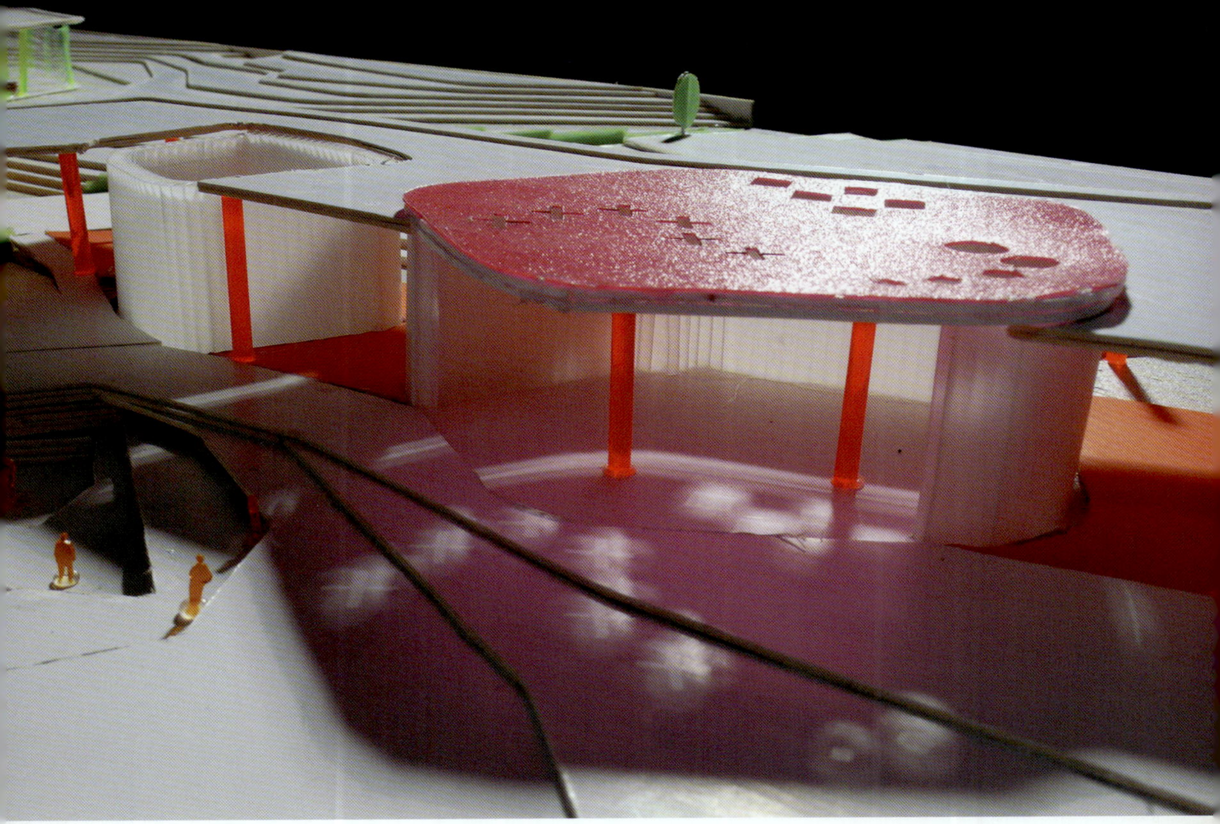

The relevance of PEP

The *POP Education Palace* seeks to interact with today's society and attract a wider public. It works on a visual and atmospheric level and offers finely-tuned spaces housing exposed as well as intimate and cosy areas. It boasts a selection of materials and colors with unique surfaces for people to see and touch. This means that *PEP* is a place that people want to experience time and again. As a result, *PEP* is an example of POP architecture because it offers spaces that can manifest these qualities.

The architecture of PEP is POP because it is a spatial and programmatic hybrid, inviting the masses into a leisure space, subverting existing power structures, and merging high and low culture.

SUPERPLAY VIDEO GAME CENTER

Andreas Bengtsson

I believe that POP architecture is about buildings which make a statement about popular culture in physical form. It should also create a footprint in the urban fabric that tells the viewer something about their function and time of construction. For this reason, the *Superplay Video Game Center* is a building designed to house video game culture. Applying the tools of POP architecture I have created an icon that seeks to celebrate and educate the public on video gaming. Thus the building uses a specific language, one that not everybody can read. It is a language for insiders (the main target group) who know and understand gaming. Everybody else will just begin by diving into a new world of architecture ...

POP and POP architecture

The *Superplay Video Game Center* is a project which tries to establish a POP architecture interpretation of the ideas found in video games. As we know, the term "POP" comes from "popular," and almost everybody would like to be popular even though not everyone wants to admit it. But there is something magic in being popular. Today, some architects strive to be popular and might just do the right thing to place architecture in a more popular spot for the masses. But why do we then never hear about POP architecture? Well, POP architecture is a genre that some say exists, and some say doesn't. POP items in music or art attract the masses, they provoke emotions, are produced in a short amount of time, and are fairly cheap to purchase. But the construction of architecture is a slow and expensive process, and the final product can hardly reach this instant connection to our hearts. All this raises a few questions. For example, is it even possible to create POP architecture by applying the same criteria used in other POP movements, merged into POP architecture? Or is POP architecture something simple, like small IKEA-style homes that you buy and use and throw away after a short period of time? Perhaps POP architecture is not at all designed and built by architects, but rather involves the participation of everybody?

Is POP architecture expressed for example in these small, temporary places that are created to serve coffee in the middle of nowhere, making everybody happy who happens to pass by?

I think that both the consumption of a product and its instant message are important if one is seeking to find the real essence of POP architecture. But as planning and construction of buildings take many years and involve many people, POP architecture must be linked to the message and the feeling a building provides over time. Therefore, to me, it is iconic architecture which is the only true POP architecture. It is architecture specifically because it is not fast to produce; and it is POP because it "talks" to the people, provokes feelings, and stays popular because it is published in the mass media, inviting everybody to have an opinion about it. And this clearly is what POP is about in the end.

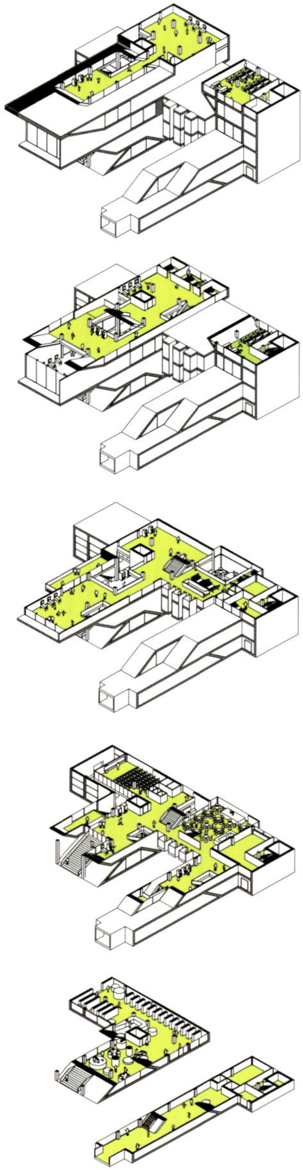

Exploded axonometries
explaining the interior system

Superplay in Berlin

The *Superplay Video Game Center* is supposed to be an icon that would give definition to the Nordbahnhof area. It is situated at the square of the Nordbahnhof station, placed between a series of shopping and entertainment buildings. This decision is based on the idea that people will come here by car or public transportation and then be tempted to visit the *Superplay Center* instead of doing daily shopping. The *Superplay Center* should be the main icon on the square and the building that gives the area its special character. It is not a highrise or a structure that is visible from afar. It doesn't need to be big, it is meant to attract the masses through its iconography. It works like a video game – once you have seen it you become interested, and then, later, addicted.

For this reason, the major POP aspect and design tool in my proposal is the use of the scenography of video games. Implementing commonly-known images and spatial configurations, the *Superplay Center* becomes a recognizable icon of the video game world. Working with rather unspecific spaces such as box-shaped rooms and staircases, the building presents the visitor with a gun-like profile and terraced spaces interacting with the surroundings, which are literal translations of graphics used in video games. The viewer who can decode the architectural shape is reminded of the zapper from the first Nintendo home entertainment system. This code allows the building to provide a kind of "Wow!" experience and an additional emotional reaction from the experts. A legible icon for the masses is the circa 6 by 12 meters LED-screen located on the front façade of the building. This screen attracts people from a distance, night and day. The screen is a direct element from the video game and becomes a mediating element between the architecture and the people. As this screen indicates, the *Superplay Center* doesn't aspire to a sophisticated architectural language. Its simplicity allows the direct communication with the masses.

In addition, the project is directly linked to the underground public transportation system. In this way, the *Superplay Center* could engage people both above and beneath the ground. Upon entering the Nordbahnhof station, people on the train key into the iconography of the *Superplay Center*, inducing them to leave the train to explore. Once inside the building, the approach of the direct interpretation of video games is continued with platforms on different levels resembling a two-dimensional video game. The idea was also that it should be harder to find your way, the higher up in the building you get. To do so I used wider stairs in the lower levels and offered only one possible way to ascend in the building.

But while the exterior is producing an iconographic sign, the inside wants to let people experience the games through the machines. There, the joystick and the computer-screen are the tools where the magic is created.

Reflection

POP is a natural part of many peoples' lives. And the presence of different genres of POP tends to give our often boring and repetitive lives extra spice and edginess. Thus the *Superplay Center* is not striving to become a global player, it is rather a test-case for the iconic, localized architecture of everyday life. In that sense, POP architecture can be a catalyst for different social or cultural groups of our time. I chose video games as the topic for this project, but it could be shopping malls, parking garages, or family homes in the future. POP architecture can start to rethink – in function and shape – these spaces which are highly criticized in the architectural scene today. Therefore, the immersion of the architect in the POP world might not only be dangerous, but also be the beginning of a valid architectural trend.

View from the city square to the main entrance

4 THE ECONOMICS OF POP

VENTURI'S REVENGE, OR HOW ARCHITECTURE WENT "POP!"

Pedro Gadanho

Roomer van Toorn recently stated that the relationship between architecture and POP is no longer about being popular but rather about creating the popular. To his proposal I would like to add the idea that architecture has in fact already been absorbed by the popular. Architecture is now a part of the scene, in fact a part of popular culture. That is, architecture is now part of the media scene. Indeed popular culture is more and more identified with what is displayed in mass-media such as MTV, life-style magazines, or daily newspapers. And one cannot deny that popular culture is also more and more entangled with consumer culture.

The burst

Architecture went "POP!" because it entered the vein of POP art, and architecture went "POP!" because its autonomy bubble definitely burst.

Today, the "popular" is what is popularly consumed. As such, even craftsmanship exists only to fulfill an exotic consumption impulse. And because, by now, architecture has spectacularly entered the fields of both mass media and popular consumption, architecture has indeed gone "POP!" But I wouldn't restrain the idea of architecture going "POP!" to its being part of popular culture as we now know it.

The first part of this proposition is easily understandable. As we know, architecture follows in the steps of art with a variable degree of delay. There are rare moments in which architecture seems to nearly catch up with art – such as when Archigram was exploring their own version of POP at the end of the 1960s. And there are moments in which the delay between art and architecture becomes truly tedious – as when minimalism is stripped of its sense and pursued like some sort of ascetic boredom.

So, after exploring the vein of minimalism for what seemed a painful eternity, architecture now decided to go "POP!" once again. After all, with its star-system all over the place and its popularity sky-rocketing, architecture truly couldn't resist going more and more "POP!" As politicians and celebrities know, popularity is addictive. As such, well-known prior priests of the strictest minimalist economy – like, for instance, the very Calvinistic Herzog & de Meuron – are now pursuing the delights of ornament and extravagant science fiction shapes. How much more "POP!" can you go?

This drives me to the conclusion that the opposition I have drawn in some of my previous writings between minimalism and diversity was somewhat wrong. I should have had the immediate insight that what historically opposed minimalism was, obviously, POP. Both art movements came up at about the same time. And both questioned art's autonomy as represented by the institutionalization of abstract painting. Both proposed that art somehow escaped the privilege of the unique artistic object and its corresponding museum context. But they had different approaches. Minimalist art created objects that focused the viewer's attention on the industrialization of manufacture and on the surrounding spatial

Galaxy Science Fiction
David Stone's cover for the first issue of *Galaxy*, October 1950

experience. POP art directly reconnected its production to the outside world of popular culture and mass consumption. Later, architecture's delayed appropriation of minimalism totally inverted this movement's premises. Retaining only minimalism's formal aspects, minimalist architecture served, firstly, to maintain architecture's autonomy principle and, secondly, to focus the gaze of the user on its beautiful boxes.

The created expectations

Yet, now that architecture has decided to go "POP!", it is to be expected that its autonomy will be continuously and intensively undermined. This will happen not only because the POP approach is the one that more effectively breaks down the barriers between high and low culture, but also because circumstances now help in making that move highly attractive. As I suggested already, being popular – and creating the popular – is something tremendously attractive.

When Robert Venturi proposed that architecture may draw from the popular visual culture of the contemporary urban landscape, I think he was truly unaware of the potential of what is actually happening today. In fact, at the time and later, he was even accused by its detractors of only using the idea of popular culture to reinforce architecture's position at the high end of the cultural spectrum.

By absorbing popular forms and images into its vocabulary, architecture would thus regain its role as the determinant of popular taste. This is partially true, and this is also what is now partially happening.

In fact, part of architecture's move towards "POP!" is related to the desire to reposition architecture, most notably put forward by Rem Koolhaas. Naturally, that yearning installs a predisposition to create the popular.

But some external circumstances and demands are also needed, and those are set by the fact that architecture has become truly mediatic. Never before has architecture been as present in the mass media as it is today. Never before has architecture's establishment been so popular and well-known. And this beginning development (i.e., success) seems to carry the potential of being increased. Although architects still complain, never before in its history has contemporary architecture been so warmly welcomed in its own time. By way of its hyperdiffusion in generalist media, architecture has not only returned to the public sphere of (consumer) society, but it has also become a very visible part of its (popular) culture. Architecture is now acknowledged by affluent Western societies as an interesting cultural and economic asset. With its symbolic capital amply recognized, architecture has thus definitely entered the realm of mass consumption. But the logic of mass consumption – as that of the mass media – imposes that one corresponds to the popularity you have created. Architecture has, by now, created expectations that have to be fulfilled.

The need to fulfill these expectations leads not only to populism, but also to architecture going "POP!" As such, architecture is going back to the vault of popular visual culture and re-offering its forms and shapes to the people in all possible versions. Iconic architecture, colorful architecture, DIY architecture, Manga architecture, monumental architecture, science fiction architecture, silk-screened architecture, Tupperware architecture, or typographic architecture ... there they all confirm this tendency. And, simultaneously, architecture also becomes a shared popular language from which other urban practices – such as communication designers or artists – are free to draw. This is what I have been calling open-source architecture. Open-source means only that the code of architecture is now shared and that architectural autonomy is thus impossible to maintain.

Architecture happily burst out into popular culture. Architecture went "POP!" and was finally freed from itself.

EXPO 2000 Pavilion
Hannover, Germany
Architects: MVRDV

HOLY-POPCROPOLI

Marta Onofre, Giulia Tubelli

Here is our story. It consists of a first part, the *Preludes*, and a second part, the *Hallucinations*. But before we start – be warned! For it is a story mostly about POP and popularity, but also about other things, too. And, you must know that our first impulse concerning POP was to use it to explore the relationship between architecture and religion. For us, POP comes to religion because religion is the only thing as popular as POP itself. Mixing the sacred (holy) and commercial functions of meaning and religion, the project takes the main theme of popular religion and transforms it, creating a religious city inserted into the heart of Berlin. After all, what is more popular in the history of the world than religion?

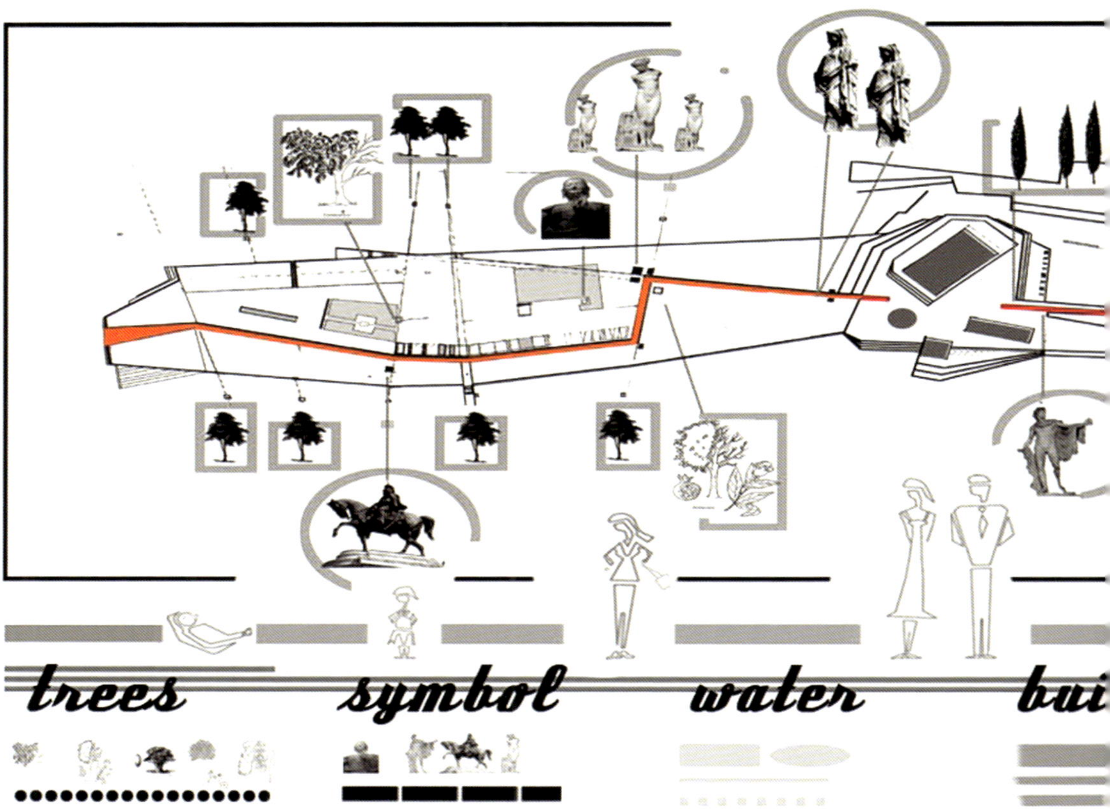

Brochure
Excerpt from the Holy-Popcropoli brochure

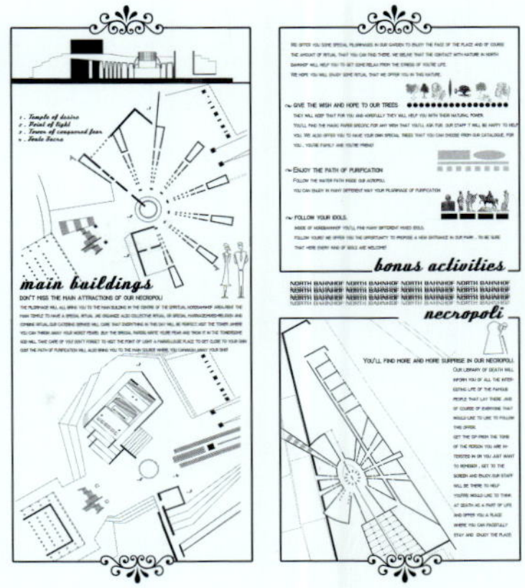

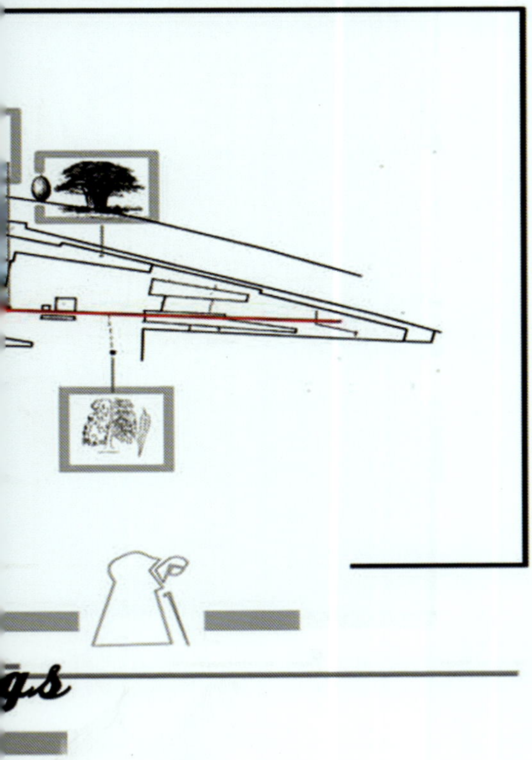

PART THE FIRST / PRELUDE(S)

Prelude 1: The story

Early on, we understood that all of our questions on POP in architecture had to do with some element of the "eternal." And we understood that we needed a place, a physical 0 contemporary site, to generate this exploration of POP. Berlin, as one of the few really international European cities, struck us as perfect for this purpose. Nevertheless, we are sensitive to the fact that this theme is complicated, démodé, and perhaps even dangerous. So we needed something more powerful and contemporary, something that, like religion, deals with the wishes, desires, and fears of the people. Also, it needed to be a business. Thus we were seeking to create a hybrid of religion and consumption, of faith, trust, and happiness.

This was our strategy: to create a holy-POP layer, and a cynic-POP one.

dreams and nightmares
mixed together
having money join spirituality

Prelude 2: Wishes

We see architecture as constructed emotional spaces. We are also interested in spirituality; this is our content, and it is the theme that architecture and religion have in common. Spiritual places are not necessarily religious, nor must they deal with a specific religion. Rather, for us, "holy" refers to places where you can feel something that your eyes can not see; they generate a precious quality, which is always, immediately, silently, close to the people. So our story is about the images and perceptions that architecture is able to create, and it is an attempt to "reload," "rework," and "reintegrate" all these images into the organic whole that is our project. For example: what happens if you collage together such core elements from architecture's spiritual ur-references as a Greek temple, a Terragni building, the ruins of Villa Adriana, the architecture of Scharoun and Barragán, etc.? In this way, we attempted to investigate the dimension of the spaces, utilizing the proportions from existing architecture in an attempt to understand the way that buildings work in relation to the built cities and the people living in them. This was the device which created the aim of our project.

Prelude 3: POP {process A}

Fears and wishes.

POP architecture must be close to the people. Thus, we named our project "POP" because it uses a strategy very similar to the one that the brands use, which plays with the fears and wishes of the people to make them need to use the architecture.

Sentimental tragedy.

We cannot offer an objective view of architecture, but rather a sentimental and tragic one. We do not brand ourselves but instead create a brand tuned to the needs of the city and its citizens. We aim to create a specific and "eradicated" space open to all possibilities but nested in the past. Thus it is critical to search all the images in the memories of the people to create a background of visual POP memories! And because it is impossible to do this in a subjective way, we can only become openly, perfectly, and extremely personal, using a "cut-and-paste" method to create our POP architecture in the same way that POP art creates its productions. Our research is oriented toward comparing architecture and religion. As we know, these two categories run a parallel path of confusion and often share imprecise instruments of representation. Therefore, it is not our goal to answer all our questions, but only to explore them using the instrument of architecture.

Shortcut.

What happens when one mixes a Romantic/personal view of architecture with a cynical/commercial point of view? What happens when one mixes the same intentions to bring people to use and get close to the architecture, but for a different basic reason, that is only concerned with money and the commercial aspect of the work of the architect? ... The holy and the profane in matrimony joined.

Typology {rules of style}.

We will not try to imitate a typology or to create our own new typology. We will not try to impose too many choices, nor will we try to justify our choices. (After all, the work of an architect is always subjective and may at times be entirely irrational.) In fact, we will try to re-elaborate the story of the images in our minds. We will allow the personal, involuntary elements of the design process their fair due, i.e., what we are, will be our architecture. (This means what we saw, what we feel, how we move; all these will be in our architecture. Inevitably.)

Typology {rules of image}.

We will allow our architecture to create images because architecture (nearly always) has something to do with the eyes. We will allow all the images created to be juxtaposed with an incredible amount of things that you have seen and felt and which maybe you also (want to?) forget.

above
Places
Necropoli's entrance
Main entrance
Forest of columns

right
Necropoli

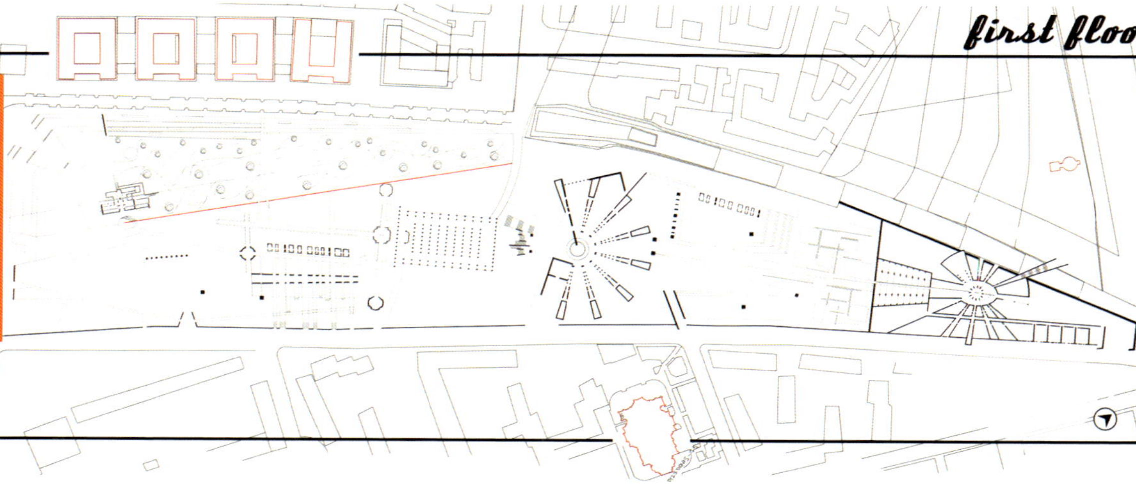

Prelude 4: POP {process B}

Acropolis reloaded.

We have taken the Acropolis hostage. But do not be afraid. We will only use it as our symbol of the memories of the collective society. It is an example of power and beauty. And it is a place where all the common knowledge and wishes of the people can become real. It is the strongest possible reference for the city and the people. It is a common place, created by people to channel the God(s). It is a place which represents culture, and in which the people are safe.

Our intention is to translate and reload the major elements of the Acropolis. But not in a didactic way. Freud speaks about the power of the Acropolis as a place resonant of the accumulations of history. We all know it as a place so immediately recognizable that, when you actually visit it, it is hard to understand that it is a real place. Because instead, you only feel guilt that your life is so short. Of course, the Acropolis is also a good example of a place where different uses of buildings (program) are integrated. And not only this, but it is also dedicated to a series of different divinities. Thus it is an excellent mixture. A hybrid symbolic city, the classic example of form and function. Yet it also works as a building, set in the contemporary city, a lived-in monument on a hill of caves, following its own rules, internal relations, and timeless context; all the while sitting in the steamy city of Athens, filled with new communal memory-seeking tourists ...

Rituals.

We are interested in rituals. They create the possibility to deepen the relationship between people, buildings, and the city. But we ask ourselves: Is a place of repeating rituals the only place where one can make rituals? Must we build rituals ...?

Context.

We use three parameters to relate our project with the context of Berlin and POP. The first is part of the process and is more theoretical and literary, while the other two deal with the scale and the proportions of the project. We have learned that in order to relate to the people, architecture must function in relation with the human body. And we know that the contemporary human body does not have the same proportions as Leonardo da Vinci's, or even Le Corbusier's

above
Holy-Popcropoli on-site

below
The main entrance

man. This is due to the fact that the perception of the world has changed since the time of our masters. The contemporary human being regularly augments his or her reality, using machines which have transformed our perception.

We are therefore forced to re-explore the question of proportions, both classical classic proportions as well as modern classic proportions. *Only* in this way can we reinforce architecture's control over the perception of the people. *Only* in this way can we give our contemporaries the fear and sense of power, the sense of the big picture, the sense of familiarity and home, and the sense of appropriate scale which today's rituals demand.

Thus the project must re-invent even the concept of proportion. We can use no existing rules. Instead, we must imagine it in our mind and in our drawings. Yet we demand proportion because we understand that it is the only way to connect the body to the building and the building to the city. When this connection is made, one can read the city within the smallest detail of the building.

History is dead! Long live history!
Our history is a trip through architecture. It is a non-linear trip with great confusion, juxtapositions, and movement. But anyway, who cares what the time is? What is important for us is the present time in which we live and in which we perceive our environment.

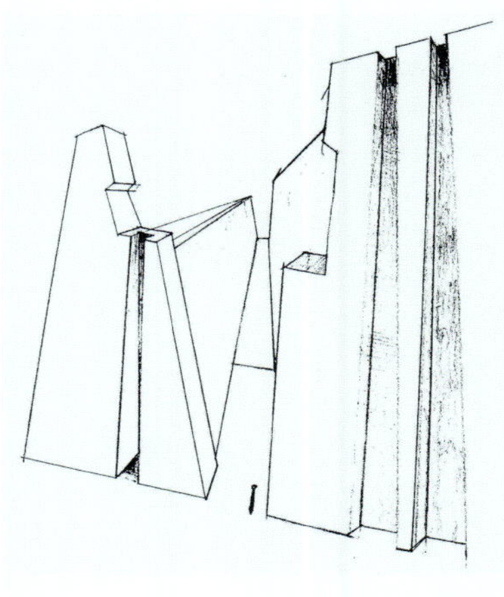

PART THE SECOND / HALLUCINATION(S)

Hallucination 1: Paths

Where are we? Maybe in Athens, maybe Agrigento, it is not so important, what is important is what is waiting for us. Does the path rise to the top of this arrogant and austere hill? It seems there is a temple, and maybe something more than this. Let's go to the city of religions, which, with her high will, is sure to bring us closer to God. The path defines the landscape and our arrival at the building; the distances within the buildings are in step with us, directly defining our perceptions about them.

Focus.

First we examine the path of perception in the landscape. We query the exact position of the aggregate of buildings, and of the buildings between each other. We explore the symbology of styling, perspectives' tricky tricks, the proportions which are offered between architecture and human.

Hallucination 2: Light

A city appears, which is defined only by light. In this city, space is the result only of the intensity and placement of lights. Gleaming and shining lights glitter all around us, a multitude of lights, little artificial stars framing big natural voids. You have seen this before, in a mosque, in an old cistern, in church, or in the last Alvar Aalto building you visited. What is important in this "lucopolis" is not where you are but rather what your experience of the space is. We must allow the light to guide us through the space and envelop us with spiritual and holy atmosphere.

Focus.

Transformation and richness of the space.
Architecture as filter of light.
Atmosphere as the creation of architecture.

Hallucination 3: Stratifying

The city stratifies the eternal. Ancient and contemporary at the same time, it is critical that we observe these hybrid conditions with care. The stratified city exists today as it has always existed. It is made of remembering and things that we have already seen, of an architecture of *déjà vu*.

Path through life
Holy-Popcropoli and its interior path designed as a path through life: from birth to death

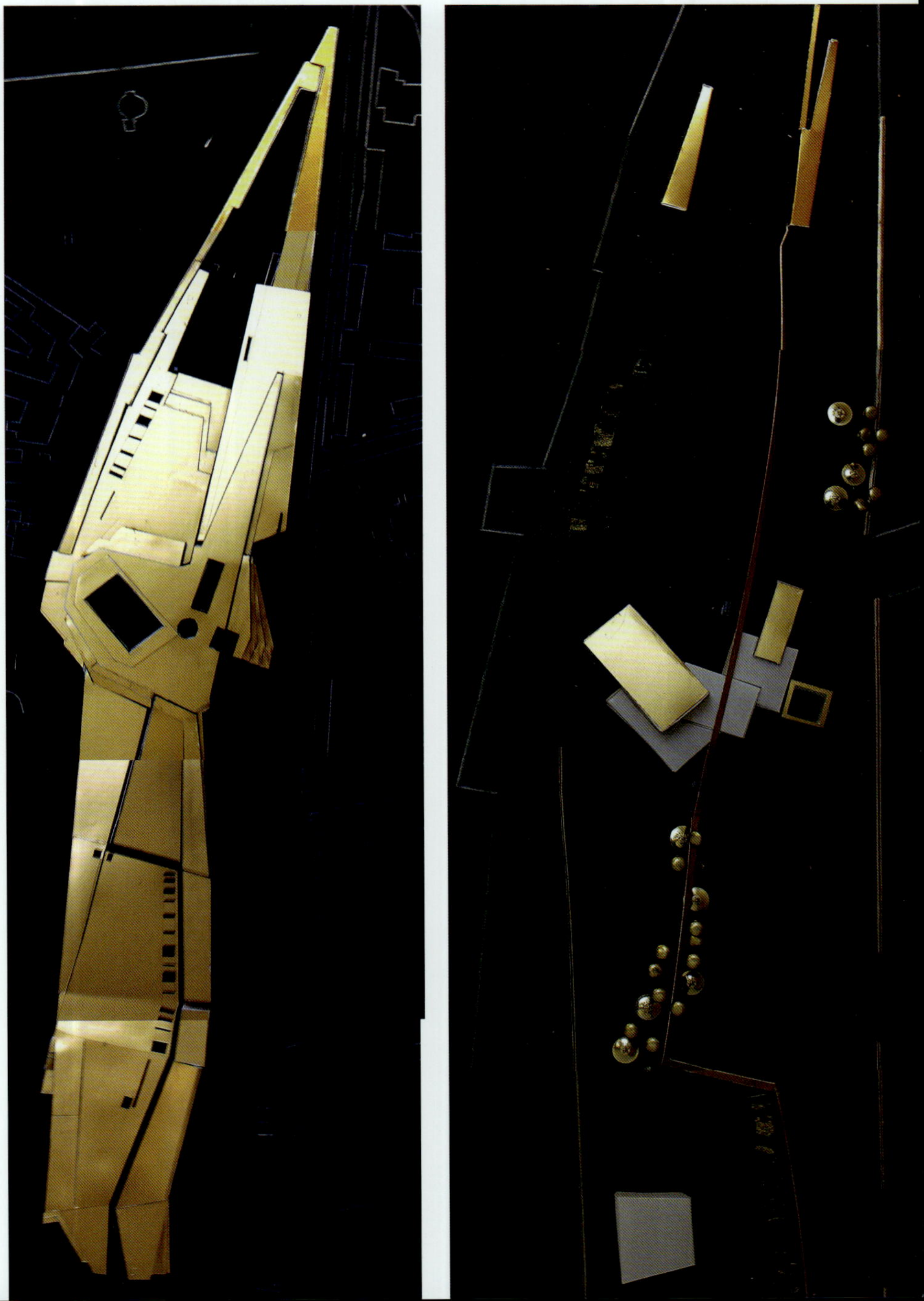

Stratum {a}.

The first image of this city, which can be an Italian city, is an image of sophisticated residential buildings in a luxury district, defined by elegant shapes and façades. The façade is a thin blade above the entrance. It reveals a symmetrical cut in which a stair is located. Within the blade, a thin gauge window tries to disappear within the façade itself. A ramp, suspended, white, in the middle of the empty basement, brings you upstairs and leads you to the flats above.

Focus.

To rework classical elements of architecture (base, window, entrance, cornice ...).

To rework the concept of the Italian palazzo.

To understand the construction of style.

Stratum {b}.

The second image is of a city or villa. The space created is one which examines the position of the major elements, which arrange the composition. The path is free and fluctuating; the atmosphere is stuck in eternal time. The materiality of the different elements are massive and eternal at the same time, as in the view from the command center of a dream.

Focus.

To explore nature and the positioning of elements.

To understand how voids create place.

Stratum {c}.

The buildings are placed as though they are big stones sitting along the street. They fight to stop time, to remember the past, and still go straight to the future. They try to define clearly the space – while still leaving possibilities for future stratifications to grow. They are lines, defining the progressive inlet into their own interiors, where space dilates with an amazing play of the section from outside to inside. We are talking about a membrane, not a wall.

Focus.

To rework the classical themes of architecture.

To reload the classical tools of architecture.

To precisely define the entrance of a building and the internal path.

Stratum {d}.

A huge stair lands here, where stratified cities meet. They are all different from each other yet resemble each other like cousins with a shared history. The statues keep it all together. They live on a different level, guiding the visitor and symbolizing outdated notions of beauty and power. Though we all know that the place cannot live without them.

Focus.

To integrate the power of symbols to manage history.

To enable memories and collective growth.

Hallucination 4: Memories and ruins

The city is completely deserted. The buildings are abandoned. If you consider ruins besides nature, inevitably they add something which no longer belongs to history. Here, time is pure. It is not burdened with history. Yet only the fellow who carefully observes the ruins can understand the meaning within.

Focus.

To understand the power of architecture to create history and territory.

Epilogue

Our journey is not finished, and never will be. As in a process of creation of POP art, in a personal way, we analyzed all the images of our banal history to re-use them in the architecture. Clearly, for us, POP means popular. Maybe what is popular today is created and consumed with extreme velocity. Anyway, what is popular is related to a catalog of images and elements which are part of the collectivity, and which likely do not come from popular culture.

We believe that the truly popular, and therefore POP, can only come from the slow and complex assimilation of concepts embedded in our minds.

The main building of Holy-Popcropoli

DESIGN EUROPE

Will Loft

Design Europe is is an architectural exploration of globalization.

Based on the concept of an ever-shrinking, ever more accessible world in which the experience of distance continues to shrink and in which ideas are generated, transmitted, and consumed at an ever-increasing pace, *Design Europe* is an agency whose mission is to disseminate worldwide the most current concepts in art and design. It is a travel agency which provides one building and location in which people and ideas can gather and converge in order to be redistributed around the world. A building from which knowledge and experience about design, art and architecture can spread. It is a tongue in cheek, blunt symbol of globalization, a signpost, its own logo and advertisement, yet at the same time it is deeply rooted in its own space and time, in its locale. The building's design has roots in that most elemental of POP themes, the re-interpretation and re-configuration of known symbols or normal objects.

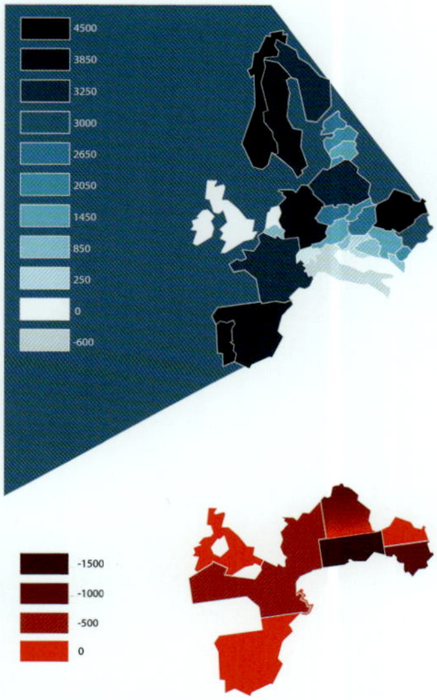

Diagram indicating the levels

Like an oversized stencil of a can of beans, a simplified map of Europe forms the footprint of the building. Unlike a two dimensional painting however, the symbol becomes stretched into three dimensions, providing usable spaces above and below the ground plane. It is a case of *function-following-form-following-function*, where the symbol becomes a part of the formal language of the design as well as providing the functional and usable spaces. The symbol is hidden from initial view and seems irrelevant to the building's interior spaces, yet as it is experienced and traversed, traveled through and understood, and the nature of the symbol becomes more and more blurred. There is no answer held within this design. The layers of irony and intrigue are directly analogous to the program within the building and the nature of POP in a globalized world. As technology and time progress, old ideas are left by the side of the road, or reinterpreted *ad infinitum* until a level of over-saturation to the point of meaninglessness is reached. New ideas, new designs, new symbols become POP and interfere with or replace our contemporary ideas and interpretations of POP.

On POP

POP is a broad-ranging and ambiguous word in modern society. It is a thoroughly amorphous concept, an idea that escapes easy categorization. As we have seen, it is a multi-use, multi-meaning word that is incredibly difficult to pin down. It often accompanies the changeable "contemporary," and resides in a similar family to "modern." The original Postmodern meaning of POP, referring to the re-evaluation of something universally accepted, becomes difficult as universally accepted norms and products are constantly changing and being reinterpreted by everyone. In some ways, the 1960s Warhol-esque POP has reinvented itself to death.

POP as popularity is becoming increasingly a quagmire of unequal numbers, where the critical mass is so over-saturated with information and constant accessibility that it is fractured into divisible segments which vie for the status of numerically "most popular." (There are so many genres of popular music now that no-one knows which is most popular any more.) The measurement of such things is so subject to the vagrancies of trend and accessibility that they are immeasurable and indeed unimportant. Their only constant is change. The same could be said of any "consumable."

Globalization is the most undeniable and obviously all-encompassing cultural phenomenon occurring within the Western world. It has the power of numbers.

For this reason I have focused on globalization. It forces movement and change, and the reinterpretation and use of the old. It is both of the above interpretations of POP.

Exterior view

Design Europe

We live in a world where the rise of the internet, cheap travel, ever-increasing technological advances, and the constant globalization of commerce have lead to a distinct bleeding of ideas and cultures between countries. This affects all areas of life. Architecture has become a global field. The way in which modern technology is blurring the boundaries between architectural stylistic norms within countries and regions allows a sort of POP style of architecture to wrestle its way to the fore. Vernacular norms give way to a sort of individualist style, where an architect's vision becomes a sort of brand, and as a consequence the forms produced in a "product form" – with which a building becomes sellable, a sort of importable identity, inherently irrelevant to place.

I have tried to bind together a number of these aspects of POP within my building, in a way that is somewhat irreverent and ironic but also distinctly localized, functional, and positive. A way that is totally relevant to site and program. This program is a stronghold of the new wave of POP architecture, a typology that has worked very hard and well for architects wishing to pursue new conceptual ideas and reinterpret a long-standing way of designing. *Design Europe* is essentially a gallery for contemporary European design, art and architecture, a cultural center of sorts for these fields of endeavor. But it is based entirely around the international, globalized nature of these fields. The gallery aims to make international design accessible to the public, to people who are unable to make the physical journey to locations with strengths in design. It achieves this not only via imported exhibitions, and via further education about the related area, but because it is in essence an enormous travel agency. People gain access to design, art and architecture from elsewhere in Europe, they gain access to information and are provided with a means to actually immerse themselves within the locations and culture whence each exhibition comes.

Essentially the program is an extension of and a tool pushing globalism even further. It works alongside the internet and the other "spaceless" elements of current globalized culture, but provides a physical point of reference, a significantly more "present" element. It is a physical location to which people can go, to actually see and experience the ideas and information inherent within the POP culture that is globalized design.

The formal tools of the architectural design work to reinforce these ideas on many different literal and figurative levels. These ideas of borderlessness, travel, movement, spread of information, speed, and ease of learning are made concrete within the actual spaces of the building through the reinterpretation of a literal and instantly recognizable form, the outline of Europe.

This outline serves as a ramp between building and park, roof for the gallery spaces, public spaces, and entry areas. It connects the intersection to the park, as well as providing public space in front of the train station. It also provides a system of navigation via ramps around a complex group of connected spaces. The materiality is derived from its surroundings and fits within accepted local norms. (Rusted steel cuts through the Berlin wall to provide entry, as in the nearby wall memorial.) These ideas are then literally rendered within the building through the requirement to journey around the spaces both inside and outside in order to not only reach the programmatic spaces, but to give a greater understanding of the building itself. The flowing roof form is only interpretable as Europe from far above (say a plane heading off on an architectural tour of the Netherlands) or, as is more likely the case, once it has been traversed by foot and the highest point has been reached, and the viewers can look down upon their path. One is able through this experience to gain a personal interpretation of the nature of this journey, as well as (via the exhibitions) larger journeys.

The architecture of *Design Europe* is an experiential journey within itself. True understanding of the forms can only be gained through multiple journeys within, around, and over the building itself. The overarching symbol becomes diluted within a journey, yet remains present at all times, adding a level of personal interpretation to the building. It is a serious intervention within the city fabric, between past and present, streetscape and park, functionality and formalism. Most of all, it is changeable. Open to the viewers' interpretation, ambiguous, and loaded. Much in the way that POP is.

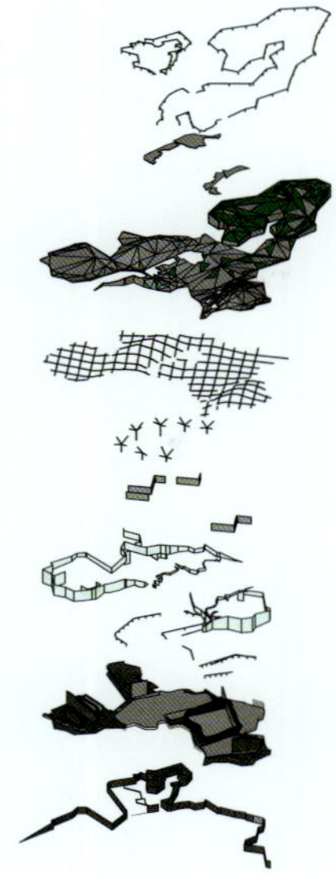

left
Space and size analysis
Use of different media
within 24h

below
Ground floor plan

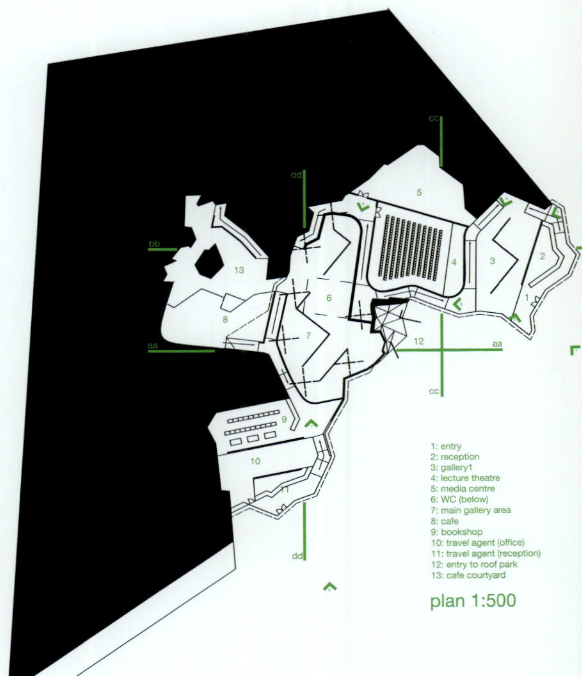

5 VISUAL POP

EXCERPTS FROM "ATLAS DER ELENDEN ARCHITEKTUR IN NORD-OST-BULGARIEN"

Iassen Markov

Introduction: What is "An Architecture of Sorrow"?

In this context, I will use the German term, *Elende Architektur,* to describe projects which exhibit both "sorrow" and "misery," meaning that they lack specific and essential properties of architecture, and – in a metaphorical sense – can also be characterized by the presence of fundamental defects or imperfections. Following are excerpts from the book *Atlas der Elenden Architektur in Nord-Ost-Bulgarien* (*Atlas of Sad and Miserable Architecture in North-East Bulgaria*) – in which some particularly poignant examples of *Elende Architektur* in Bulgaria are analyzed.

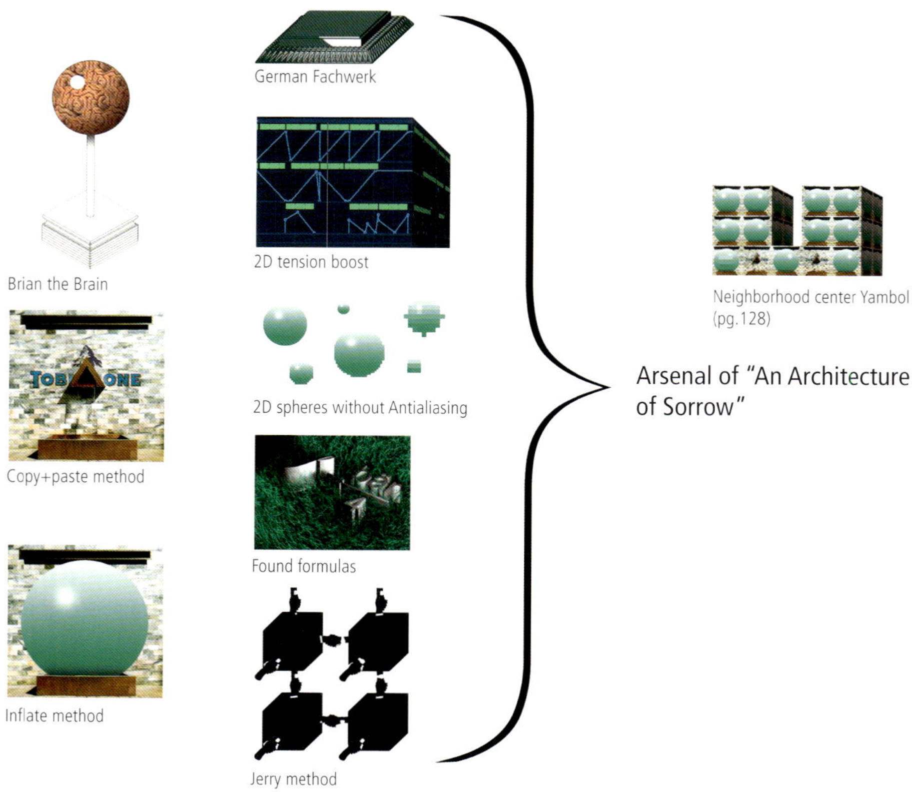

The *Elende Architektur* of North-East Bulgaria is a unique 2D architecture. Ignoring an entire dimension and reducing spaces to 2D surfaces has liberated architecture from the massiness of volume and has enabled the creation of new light-made architecture (*Leichtbau*). These pure, 2D buildings can be designed and built within an incredibly short time-frame. Therefore, the amount of *Elende Architektur* increases very fast, and – as there is not enough space for it in Bulgaria – new locations for the erection of this kind of architecture in other parts of the world are desperately required. In *Elende Architektur* details are used to create narrative, rather than constructive 2D compositions. In fact, they rather describe the processes used by the creators to arrange a 2D composition. Thus the final compositions are not evaluated by examining their functional or aesthetic qualities, but instead by exploring the arrangement of their operations, i.e., their plot or story. And of course, there are great story-tellers among the architects of *Elende Architektur* in North-East Bulgaria.

Operational knowledge

Some methods of operation within the field of *Elende Architektur* are:

1// *The copy+paste method.* The most direct creative tool to design *Elende Architektur* is the copy+paste method. It works according to the slogan "after a thousand times a lie becomes truth!" Some very good creators of the *Elende Architektur* start from a single pixel, multiplying it to create megapixel monster-structures.

2// *The inflate or scale method.* If the copy+paste method doesn't provide the wanted result, the creators of an *Elende Architektur* project may use the inflate method: inflate until it POPs! This method is inspired by Jim Morrisson. (In architectural scale 5:1 they got the guns and we got the numbers.)

3// *Fachwerk.* From a construction point of view, 2D architecture is very unstable. Therefore, German *Fachwerk* is often applied on the façades of the *Elende Architektur* to introduce stability. This kind of ornamental strategy is especially popular for governmental buildings.

4// *The antialiasing (bad zoom) method.* Good antialiasing requires high calculation performance. Unfortunately, it is not very popular there. Instead of bicubic interpolation they use simpler methods based on the definition of the closest neighbor. A result similar to a very poor zoom method is achieved. In this way the creators of the *Elende Architektur* work with narrative pictures exhibiting miserable resolutions, and revealing a feeling of lost sadness.

5// *The Jerry method.* The most important and comprehensive method of the *Elende Architektur* is the so-called Jerry method. In a paranoic-narrative delusion the story of a victim named Jerry, who has an accident while staying in a building, is being told. In the course of the story the creator of *Elende Architektur* develops the building programmatically. For the sensitive North-East Bulgarian people the sad story of Jerry is visible on the façades of the buildings. And every visitor to a small North-East Bulgarian town can fall in love with the tragedy of the *Elende Architektur*.

Perspectives

Elende Architektur is a soap-opera-architecture: accessible for both housewives and architects reading *Baumeister*. The qualities of this kind of architecture are the following: poor proportions, no perspective, and a speed of production which equals the speed in which it affects people. The dreariness in the façade and plan design are ideal characteristics for the export and worldwide compatibility of *Elende Architektur*. Essentially, the only important local prerequisites for *Elende Architektur* are accessories which suit the geographical place, such as *ficus*, cat, pool, or a nail on the wall ...

1. Elendes Zusammenhangswissen

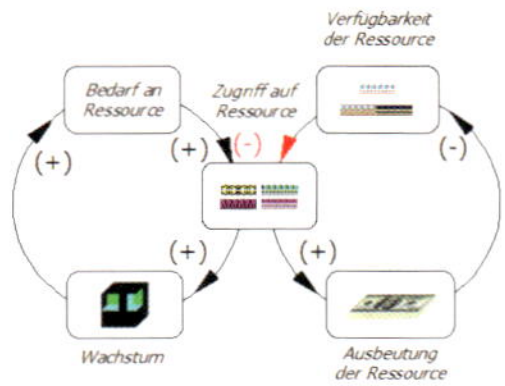

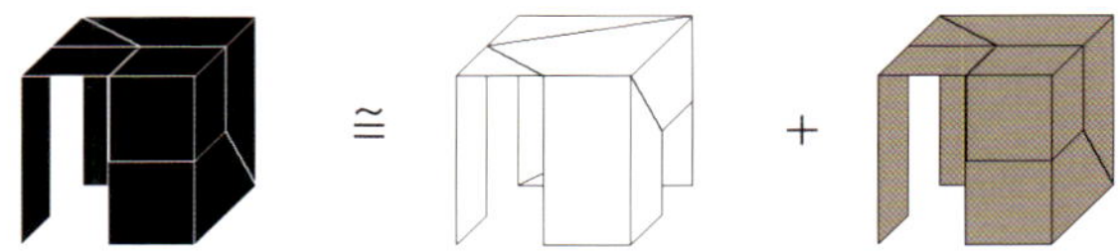

Paranoic correlation-handshake-equation ——— =

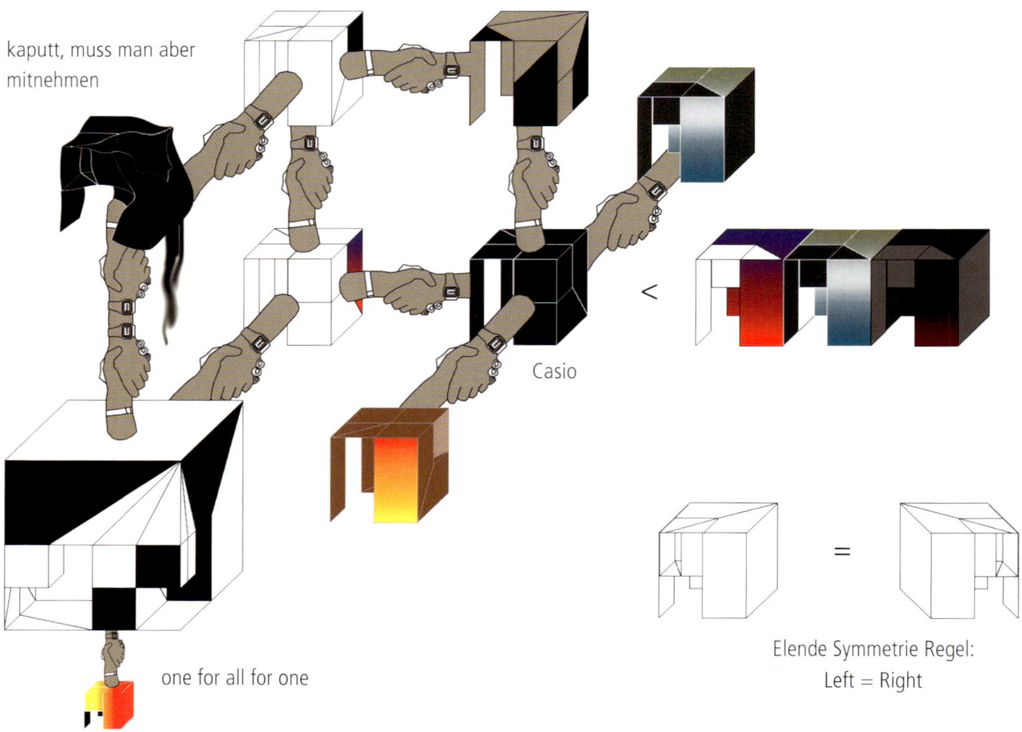

Elende Symmetrie Regel:
Left = Right

2. Elendes Ergebnis: Import-Export

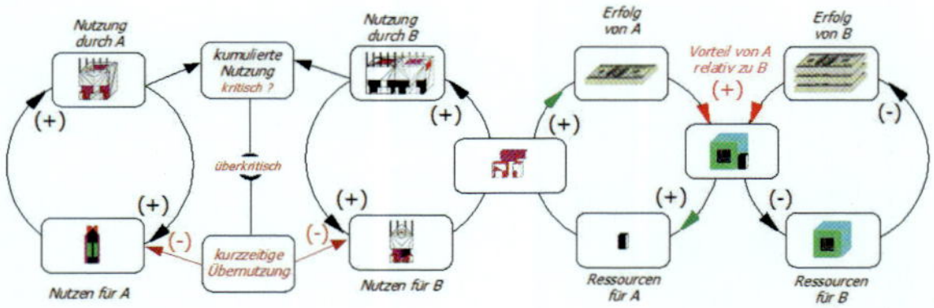

System:
If something doesn't work with money, it works with more money.

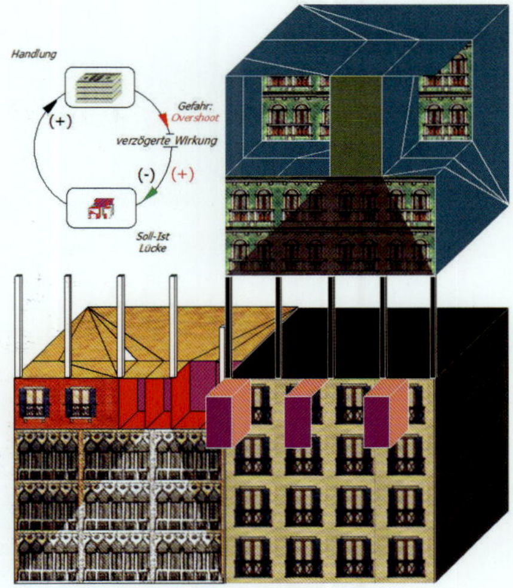

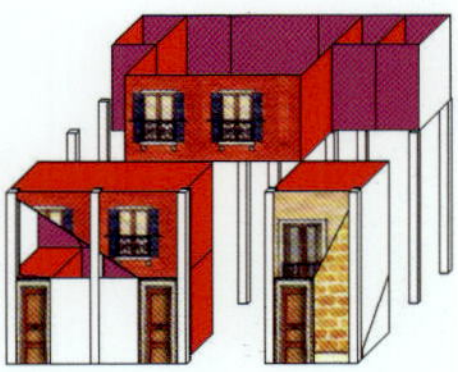

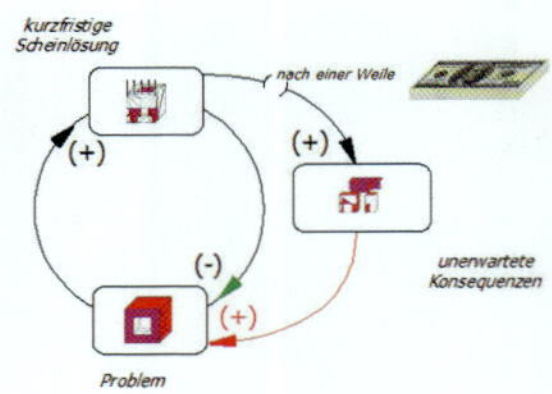

Venezianische Villa für 3 reiche Leute

Venezianischer Palazzo neben venezianischem Sozialbau

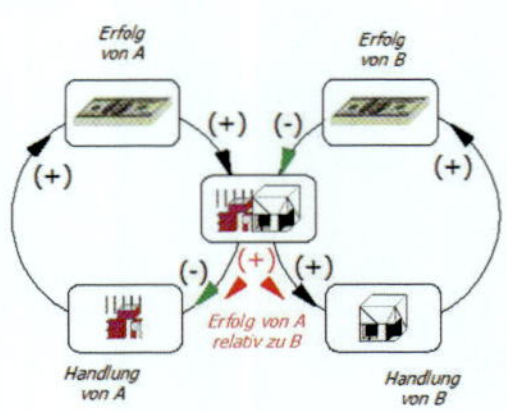

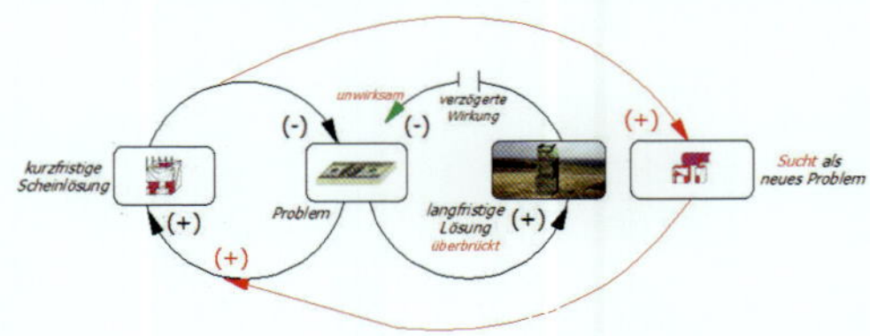

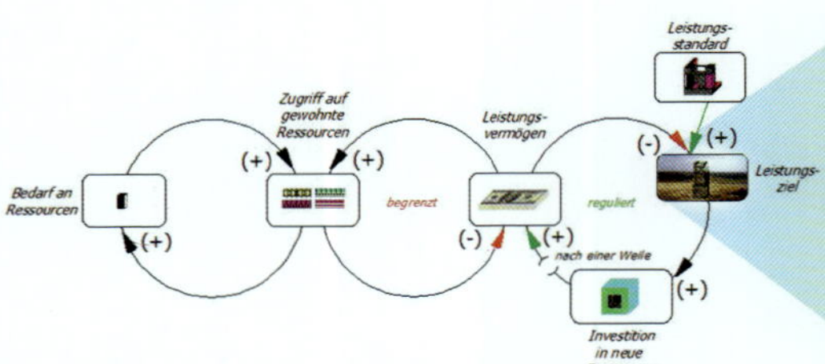

Mathematics+Sadness = Moldavian Architecture

3. Grundlagen des Fragmentwissens

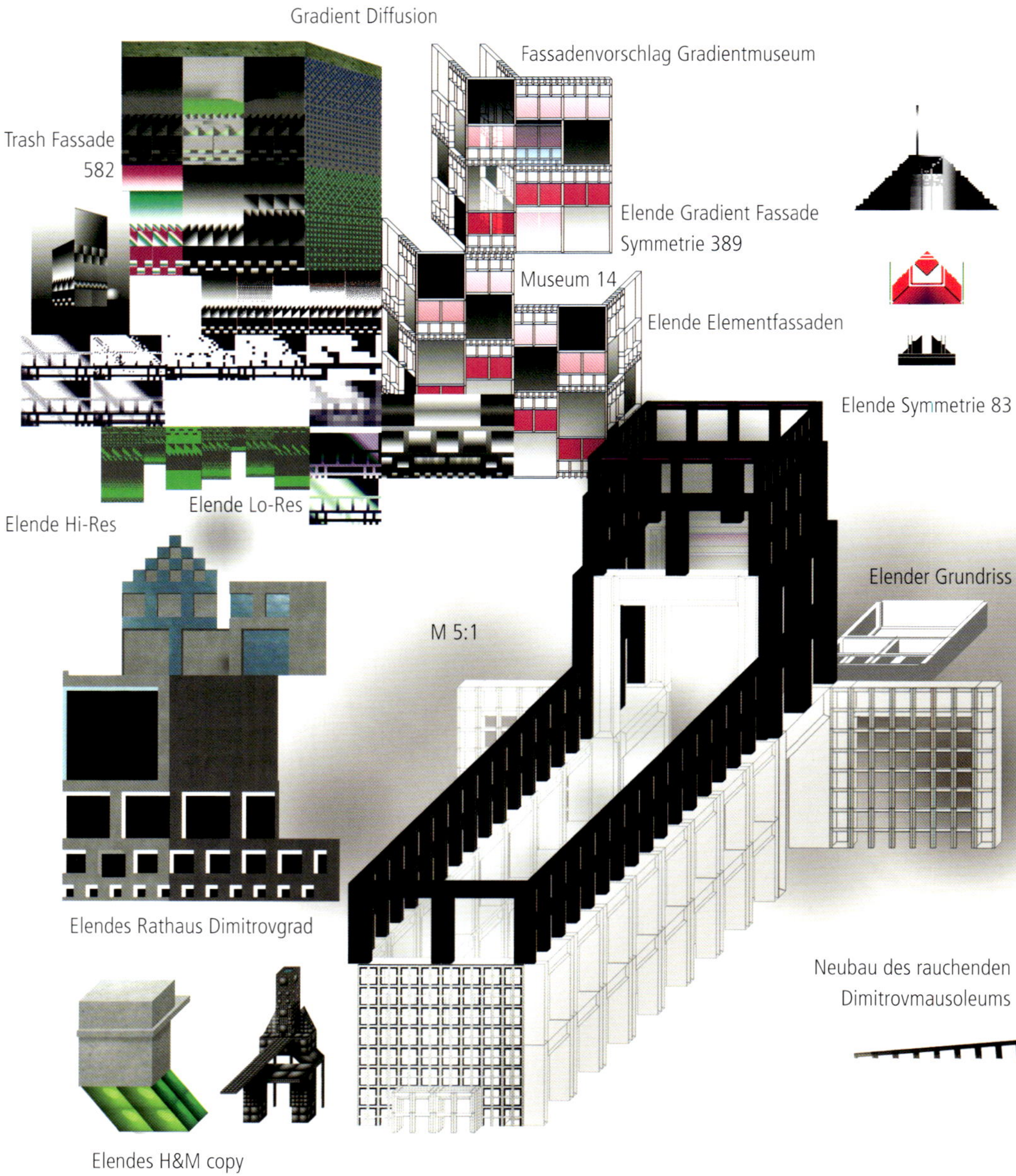

4. Elende Exportschlager

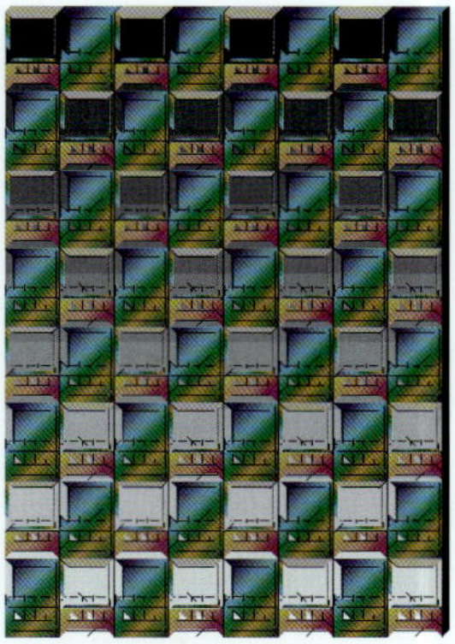

Elende Fassade 13

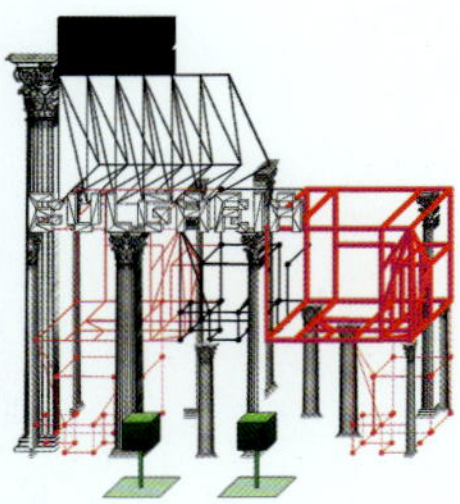

Bule Pavillion Biennale 16

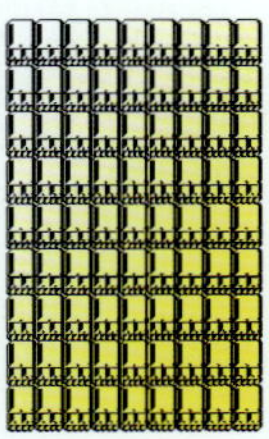

Elende Fassade 94

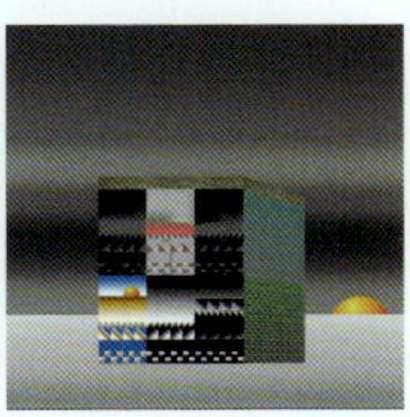

Universalfassade für Stuttgart-West und Tampere

ZITTY HOUSE

Carlos Gor Gomez, Valle Medina Ibáñez

Far from an elegant image or a stiff attitude, our project is the result of a customization process. We believe that POP is everywhere. It is part of our everyday life. Just take a look at how POP music works in that sense. You experience concerts where your favorite POP star is spectacularly endowed on center stage, and seems totally out of reach. But at the same time you are able to identify with the often very clear and direct language that appeals directly to your senses and leaves you with the impression that this person on stage is referring to real-life issues from your own life, and even that he or she might be referring to your personal situation. The combination of very clear and somewhat spectacular semiotics with down-to-earth experiences is what makes POP such an interesting phenomenon. Something eye-catching and easily accessible that involves us every day ...

POP architecture clearly needs to engage in the idea of a visual signpost as well as a mutual spacial and programmatic experience.

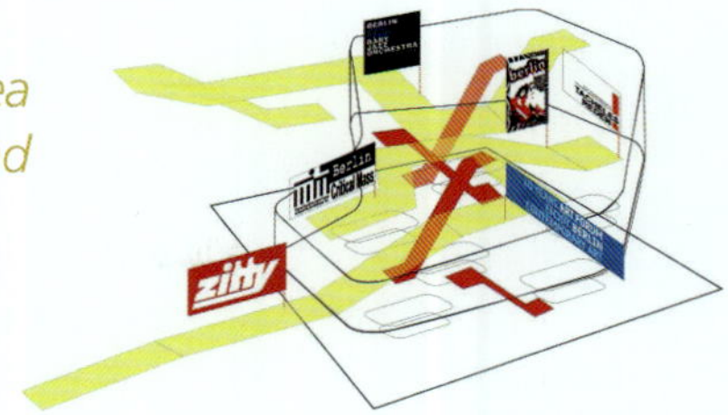

Program development
The content of the bi-weekly magazine *Zitty* is the fountainhead for our programmatic spaces.

Creating a "Berlin" image

The concept of the eye-catching and easily accessible object projected on architecture means for us to generate an iconographic image from various daily programs and functions. Therefore, POP architecture, according to us, needs to work on the exterior as well as the interior of a building.

The brand we found most suitable for our approach is *Zitty*, the bi-weekly magazine which covers Berlin's cultural scene. It also include listings for concerts, plays, movies, interesting events, and places to go to. Basically, it is a complete guide to multidimensional city-entertainment that works on different levels – from a global view on the city, via a city-specific scale, to very small units that in the end form the city, creating the image of Berlin that is being transported through the magazine. Thus, *Zitty* provides a very direct and representative description of today's POP culture in Berlin. This is why we used it to form the basis for our approach to the project. To translate these ideas into architecture, we developed a strategy that enables us to work with POP aspects from the large-scale city context down to small functional units, which in the end add up to the complete image. In detail this means we have divided our project into four scales, or levels – XL, L, M, S.

XL – Semiotic level

Here, we seek to create a new urban cultural icon for Berlin.

Naturally, the XL-level defines the scale with the widest context. POP needs to work on a large scale to communicate with the wider public. Thus, the XL-level is our major tool for addressing the masses, the city-dwellers as well as the tourists. Berlin is the site for our POP intervention, and rather than limiting ourselves to the Nordbahnhof, we chose to design a building that reaches to the city boundaries. As the exterior shape and the façade of a building are the first signs and the major communicators with the surroundings, they become a crucial element in our design. To create a new urban icon, we based the design of the exterior on semiotics that reflect the cultural complexity of Berlin as it is symbolized to us. To transport our message we used the semiotics of today's information culture – news boards and stores whose surfaces can be sold for advertising, or media publicity form the outer shell of the project.

But to become a new recognizable and memorizable icon, the *Zitty House* not only needs to have a notable and memorizable façade, but also a certain height. In this way it begins to form a new skyline for the area, functioning as a signpost and orientation landmark even from greater distances. And once you approach the building you understand that it functions as a catalyst within its surrounding urban fabric.

The commercial façade
providing information the same way a news board does

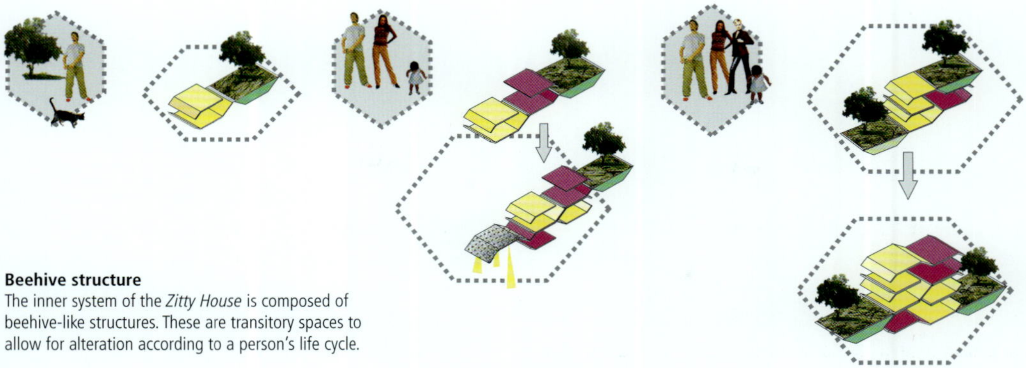

Beehive structure
The inner system of the *Zitty House* is composed of beehive-like structures. These are transitory spaces to allow for alteration according to a person's life cycle.

L – Context and program

The new Zitty House needs to indulge in its surroundings, becoming an easily accessible "street project."

The L-level is concerned with the integration of the project into the city. Thus it works with the adjacent situation, the actual site, and its surroundings, rather than with the overall city of Berlin. From our analysis of the local environment, we developed the idea of connecting the different spaces of context, joining the Nordbahnhof, the park, and the new project. A new artificial topography is generated: The building is hidden inside itself, unfolding to the outside in order to turn visible once again. This phenomenon generates a particular dialog between street territory and architecture. It is an artificial and elevated surface: a gardening roof that connects the building and the park activity in a functional, but more importantly, in a visual way. The lower part of the building as well as the tower follow the image of a "vertical street" with public gardens, and in this way draw the given and familiar urban structures into the building. Thus the *Zitty House* works both with common sense as well as with the spectacular.

M – The inner system

The inner part of the building is filled with modifiable spaces. It is like "a body without organs." [Deleuze and Guattari]

The M-level determines the overall structure and shape of the project's interior space. Here, we work with multilayered levels stacked on top of each other, and ephemeral spaces offering different cultural activities.

Gilles Deleuze and Félix Guattari discussed the term "body without organs" in their book *A Thousand Plateaus*. They use the term "body without organs" in an extended sense to refer to the virtual dimension of reality in general: "(...) This body without organs is permeated by unformed, unstable matters, by flows in all directions, by free intensities or nomadic singularities, by mad or transitory particles." Translating this description in our own terms, and using it as a basic understanding for organizational potentials, the whole architectural and organizational system of *Zitty House* is based on a bionic structure. Like a beehive, it is made of countless small units that create the inside flow through a clear but adaptable organization system.

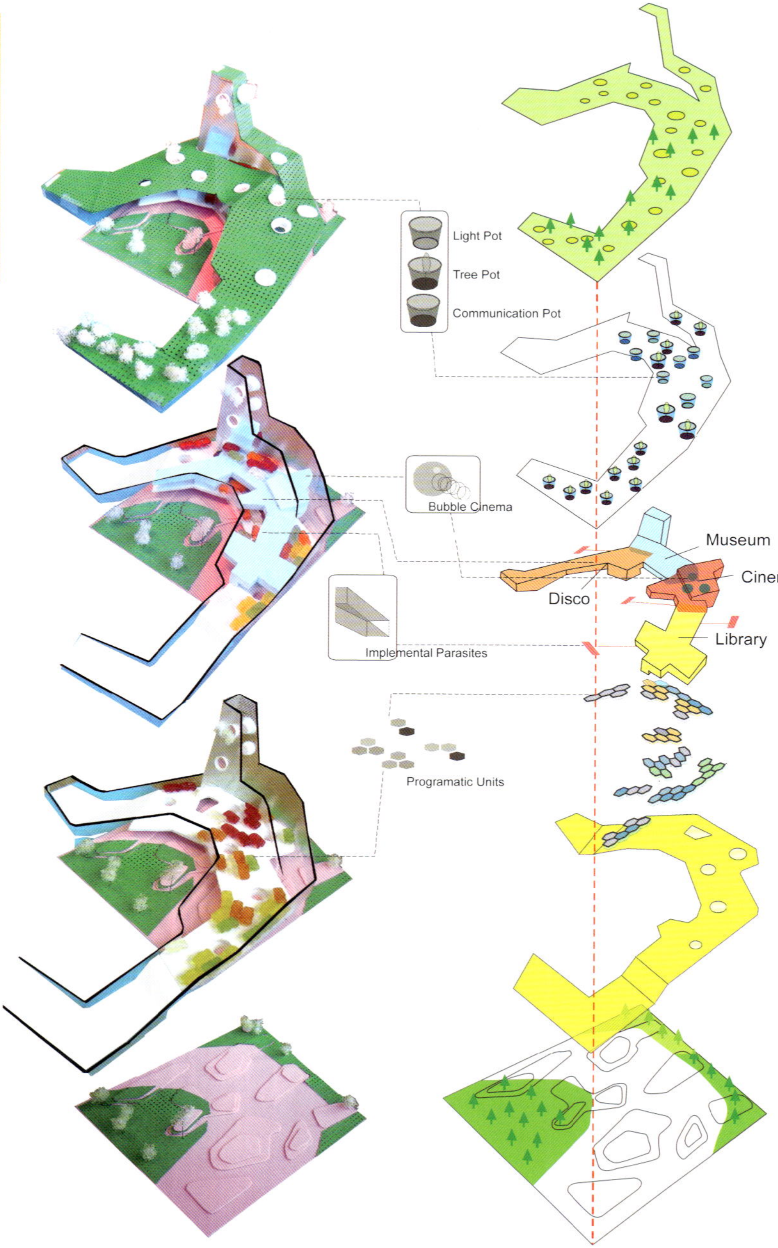

PUNCHED ROOF

Outside and inside interact with each other. The adjacent park continues as a green roof on top of our building. Different kinds of holes allow for spatial connections.

POT STRUCTURE

Various relationships between the inside and the outside exist. The different kinds of "pots" punch little holes into the building and provide a realtionship between the different building levels.

INTERNAL BODY

The internal body serves as a large public space. The implemented program is meant to attract the wider public.

FUNCTIONAL UNITS

STRUCTURAL PLATFORM

A mulitprogrammatic platform with a generous offer in the informal public area.

INTERACTIVE PUBLIC SPACE

Landscape and built structure coincide.

Volumetric studies
Development of the L-level

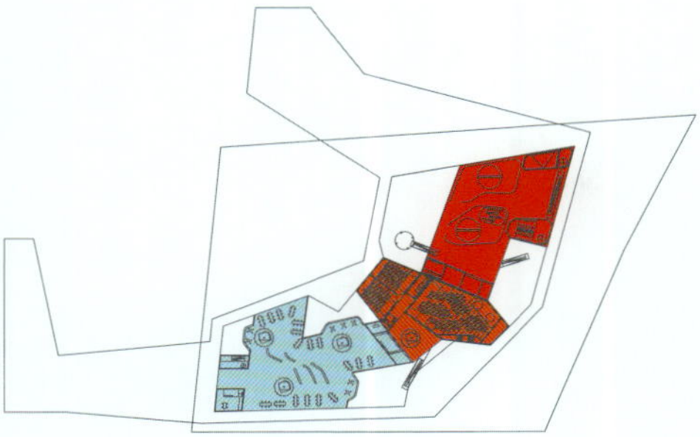
Program diagram, second floor

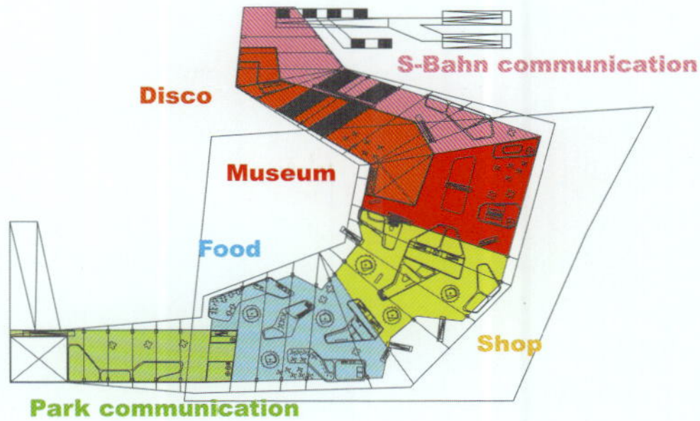

Program diagram, first floor

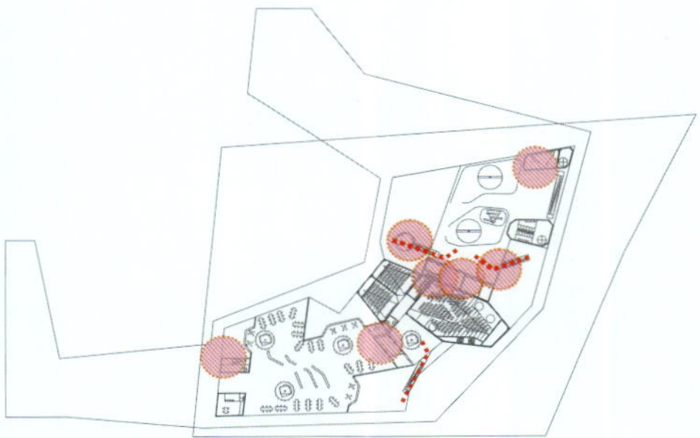
Movement diagram, second floor

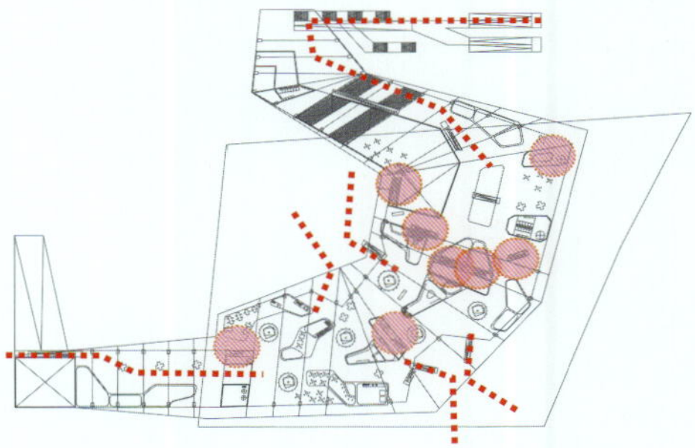
Movement diagram, first floor

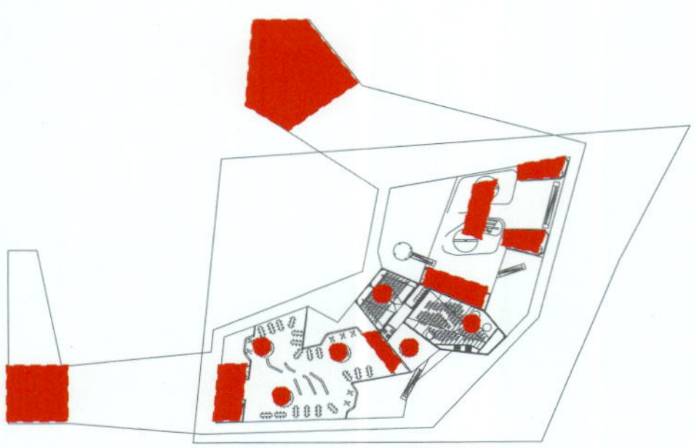
Structural system diagram, second floor

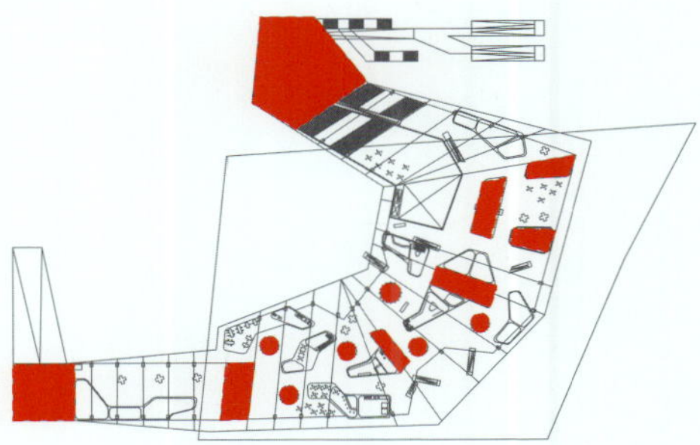
Structural system diagram, first floor

Diagrams
Development of the M-level

S – Customized architecture

All spaces are designed so that users can modify them on a daily basis or use them in a personal way; shops, libraries, a cinema, gardens, ...

The S-level is the smallest scale inside the *Zitty House* – the human scale. Every space within our structure can be customized and transformed by the visitor to fit his or her personal needs. All spaces are to become public in the sense that visitors can participate in the mutation of the internal order. The flexible system of the project creates spaces for multi-programmatic functions, be they hanging gardens, housing units, shops, discos, or movie cells. These activities are reflected on the outside of the building through its multimedia façade.

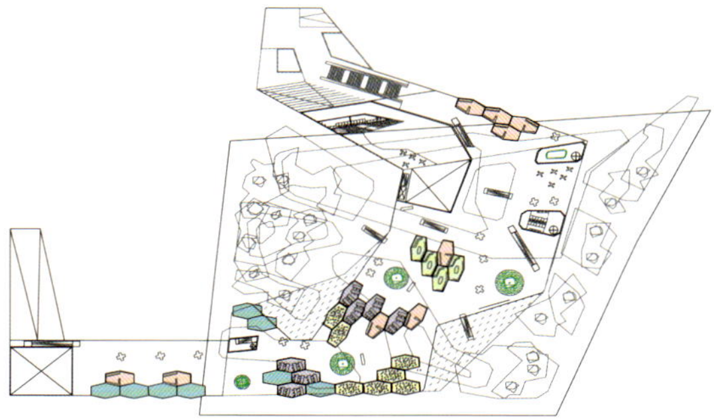

top right
Floor plan

bottom right
Façade
Unfolded drawing

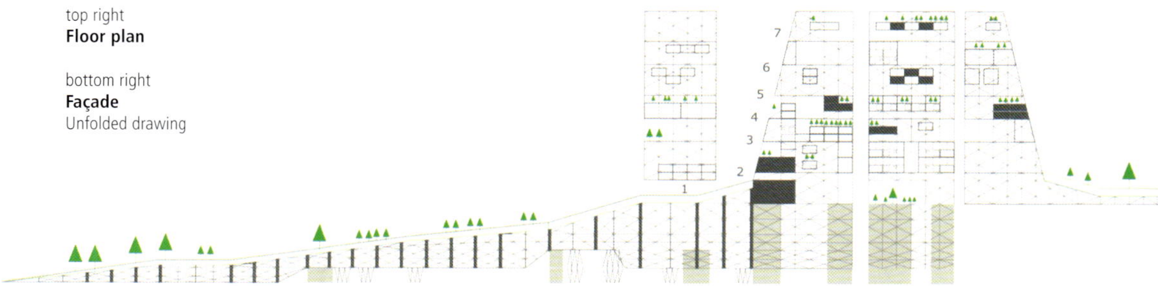

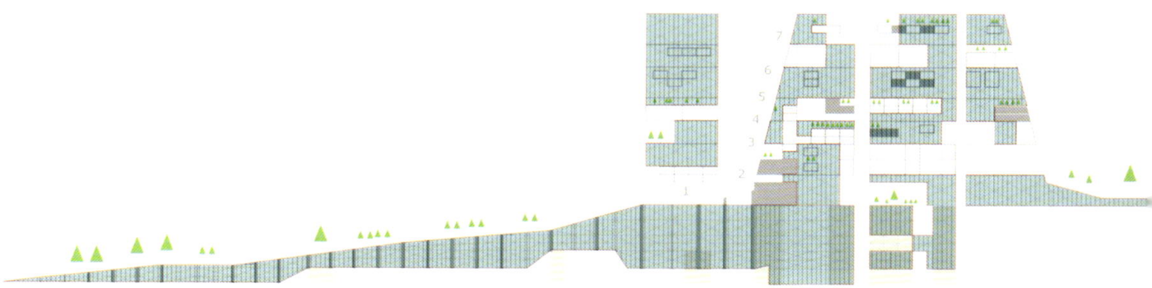

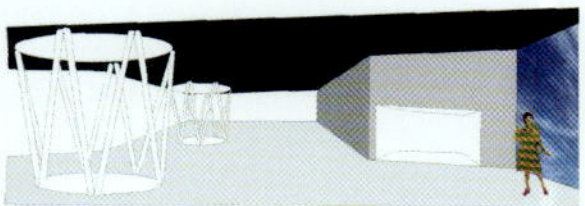

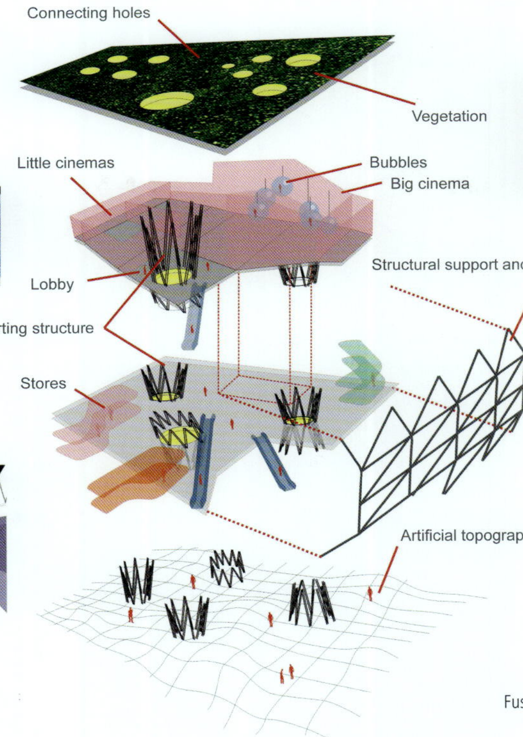

Exploded view
Fusion of program, structure, and form

The POP factor

The cultural phenomenon POP works on a series of levels within our project. But for us, the visual level is the most important, because it is the one which we think actually communicates with the environment, being the most accessible and identifiable. Therefore we believe that the general public speaking of architecture mostly just considers the appearance of a building. With the *Zitty House* we seek to introduce other nuances, woven into the different scales and levels of the concept; i.e., the iconic function of the spectacular *Zitty House* tower within the city, the easy approachability of the new complex because of its sensitive implementation in the urban context, and the chosen popular functions. Further, there is the possibility of one-to-one interaction with the internal space, which will then be projected through the façade and again interacts with the city. In a similar way to how the magazine *Zitty* reflects Berlin on different levels, we want to generate a phenomenological project. While some places or activities will start to influence people in their choices, magnetize the masses, and become POP, others will lose their attraction.

Like the magazine, the Zitty House aims to achieve a complex integration and interaction with the city and its habitants in order to play an active role in reflecting and defining Berlin. Then it can become part of our everyday life. It can become POP.

LECKERKNECKE CRISP BREAD CENTER

Martin Hartwig

LeckerKnecke is a bread-producing company which is planning to construct a new branding center – the *LeckerKnecke Crisp Bread Center* – in the heart of Berlin, where many families and young people live. Huge fields of newly-planted wheat will reach toward terraces on the building, providing space for picnics and relaxation. Food and picnic supplies can be bought in the small organic food store or the café of the *LeckerKnecke Crisp Bread Center*. The architecture of the building refers to the shape of a wheat spike, expressing the company's corporate identity. But the main attractor for the public will be the healthy, golden shiny image of wheat fields, creating a large rural-like and picturesque public space in the heart of Germany's capital city.

View from the wheat fields

POP strategies as a marketing tool

Quality products alone are often not enough to help companies thrive in our harsh capitalistic economy. Rather, today's businesses are more and more dependent on their customer's loyalty, seeking ways to construct a strong corporate identity which binds clients to their products and thereby helps them survive competition with other market players. This approach has been recognized and practiced in all areas of corporate development and advertising. And now, once again, architecture has become a popular and powerful tool to help transport a clear and recognizable image for a brand. Rather than using vague associations such as "high-tech" or "futuristic," buildings can help to transport a unique and unmistakable image of a brand.

Such is the case with the *LeckerKnecke Crisp Bread Center*. Here, the project's strength lies not so much in a POP building itself as in its embedment within a unique inner-city landscape. The mere size of this open field and the courage of the company to leave it untouched transports a statement that can only succeed in POP aspects.

LeckerKnecke has decided to use a very simple but strong image to broadcast their corporate identity – a wide field of beautiful wheat plants that wave in the wind and into the mind of the consumer ...

POP architecture has the ability and power to refer directly to people's senses and provoke emotional associations.

The huge site is almost entirely given back to the people as public space. It is perennially accessible, appealing to lovers of today's trendy organic food as well as all other citizens. To the broader public the image of the golden shiny wheat fields will be the memorable signature of *LeckerKnecke*. The extraordinary concept of turning such a central place in Berlin into a spectacular rural area manifests a strong and clear statement in the cityscape. While the company profits from the implementation of firm-associated signs and offers, the city profits from a newly defined public space. The *LeckerKnecke Crisp Bread Center* will be a new icon within the city of Berlin, attracting many people and making the company more popular.

The LeckerKnecke Crisp Bread Center

LeckerKnecke is an imaginative and healthy company dedicated to producing food products from crops, like crisp bread, corn flakes, and various kinds of bread. The company is currently trying to increase its popularity with a new branding center in the capital of Germany. Products of *LeckerKnecke* are sold in organic food and exclusive department stores and selected supermarkets. Young couples and families belong to the main target group of *LeckerKnecke*. The typical *LeckerKnecke* client has an average or above income and is strongly interested in healthy food. This target group is found in the direct neighborhood of the site, in Berlin Mitte and Prenzlauer Berg. Generally, the site around the Nordbahnhof is an ideal location for the *LeckerKnecke* company, as it is in a central and upcoming area that was Berlin's "no-man's-land" during the period of the city's division. It has not been developed since.

Site model
In the huge empty space in the heart of Berlin a spectacular wheat field is embedded.

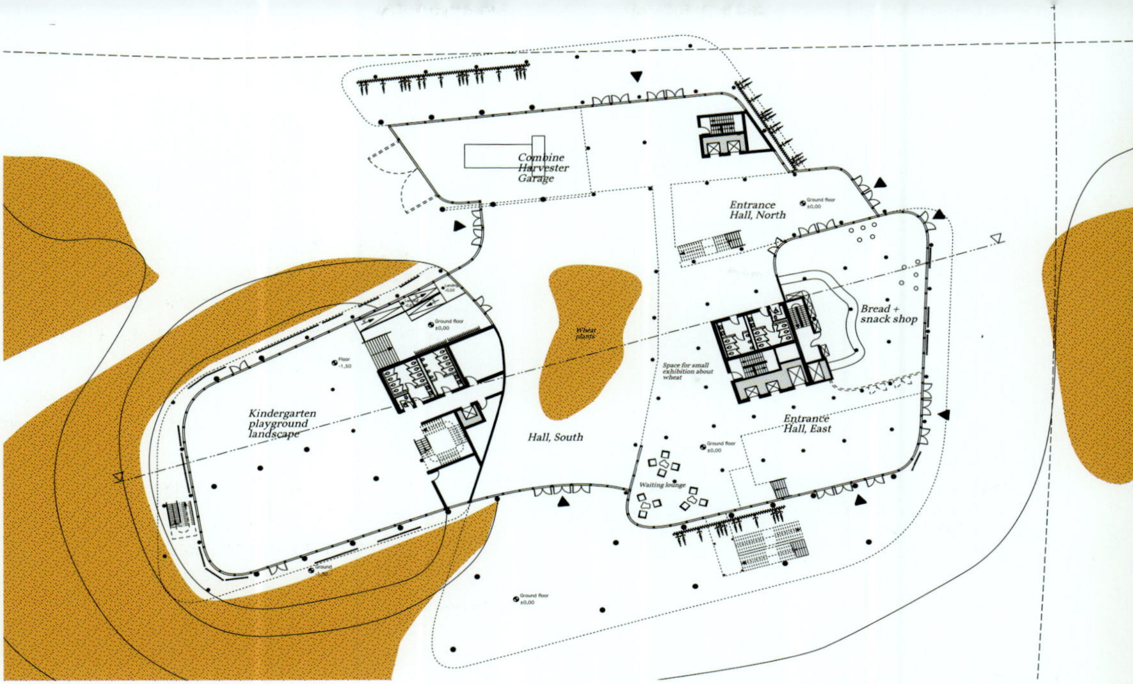

Ground floor plan

As wheat is the basis of most *LeckerKnecke* products, the image of wheat plants and wheat fields defines the corporate design of the company. A fresh wind softly blows over the fields – a shiny golden color from the sunlit wheat projects a healthy, fresh, and joyful atmosphere.

The image of "waving wheat fields" transports the company's "feeling" strongly – proving a nature-orientated attitude and promoting an image of freedom.

The growth cycle of the plants will change the surface of the space continuously and will allow people to take part in this agricultural process, with its peak at harvesting time when the monstrous harvester – otherwise parked in the lobby of the *LeckerKnecke Crisp Bread Center* – will crop the shiny golden brown fields, and the whole neighborhood will join in the year's most expected event. It is the POP simulation of the traditional village harvest ... Crossing the wheat fields one gets the chance to enter the main building. Thin vertical wood panels on the façade of the *LeckerKnecke* building create a constantly fluid movement. The building serves peoples' needs by providing products from the bakery or the organic food store, enjoying a wheat coffee in the restaurant or other leisure and entertainment facilities presented. Furthermore, the building offers its visitors the chance to change perspective and step up to one of the terraces or the top level. With the elevation over the ground the impression of the wheat fields changes, revealing an unrestricted view. The overall extension of this rural-like inner-city landscape becomes clear for the first time. This extraordinary scene leaves a convincing and attractive image in the visitor's mind and will persuade him or her to come back and take advantage of *LeckerKnecke's* unique, hybrid urban-rural landscape.

6 POP – REINTERPRETED

PLASTIC COATED GLADE – POP INTERVENTIONS OR BRUTUS REX

Kai Magnus Bergmann, Uta Böcker

PLASTIC COATED GLADE – POP INTERVENTIONS OR BRUTUS REX

Kai Magnus Bergmann, Uta Böcker

Today, architecture and POP are inseparable.

The current generation of architects promotes architecture as a product free of the ideological chains of the past. An increasing number of architects want architecture to be easily understandable, quickly consumable, and preciously adored. Of course, popular buildings have always existed in one form or the other. We consider all of them as built manifestations of the preoccupation with their outer appearance. Thus the most powerful tool a POP architect has at his or her disposal is the façade, which forms the first impression. Furthermore, POP is about individual pleasures, fantasies, and mass accessibility.

Our intention has been to work with these characteristics of POP and to implement a POP intervention on the site of the Spreepark, an abandoned amusement park in East Berlin. This site can be considered a lament for a vanished POP culture.

It is characterized by
Melancholy,
Romanticism,
and long-lost Pleasures ...

POP stories

At the beginning there was our site, the Spreepark: fascinating, mystical, and abandoned – located directly on the river Spree in the south-east of Berlin. Vacant since 2002, it was forgotten save for being occasionally photographed by sauntering pedestrians. After the fall of the Berlin Wall the amusement park was taken over by a West German investor who scuttled the once prestigious DDR leisure park within the briefest time, and under shady circumstances. The site would have faded away from the public's memory, if it was not for the giant Ferris Wheel. Effortlessly, the 45 meter high structure tops the trees on the banks of the Spree and is visible from far away, even from the Oberbaumbrücke, an inner-city bridge. This Ferris Wheel acted both as the Spreepark's and as the city's landmark. It gave pleasure to the people and marked the DDR's little place of joy even from far outside. It was long an important symbol of POP culture – and it should remain that way.

We believe in POP as a phenomenon comprehensible for everyone, but allowing especially for individuality. POP is for the masses, serving to entertain and working against mournfulness. We find POP everywhere, and it is an adequate expression of our daily lives. To an extreme, we found an objectification of these POP characteristics in the fun-rides, the buildings and landscape design of the former Spreepark area. By having studied the relation of POP and architecture, we wanted the site to be both, utilized in an extremely popular way, and giving consideration to its established and preserved POP spirit. We were interested in an intervention that leaves space for the site's peculiar identity, which, desperate for attention, needed to be acknowledged and above all protected via a strategy centered on attracting the public's interest. Thus our intervention seeks to re-introduce it to the people and make it loved once again, so that a new identity can emerge. In our opinion, the contrast between decaying fun-rides and the general tarnishing makes the old hypertrophic and allows the new to create a contrast to the existing parts by its outer appearance. We deliberately wanted to create a functional patronage of the old through the new.

We found a manifold cadaver of POP – a pile of trash that remained from the old park. However, it was fair and beautiful.

Based on our fascination with the site's existing conditions, we deliberately decided to support and celebrate nature's overgrowing of the park. Thus our project, *Brutus Rex*, implements modern housing units offering generous living spaces and privacy within its exiting structure. The implementation of green areas adjacent to the apartments aims to exaggerate the theme of the overgrowing park at unified odds within the new structure. The volumes of the structure were devised out of the old carnival rides which, through subjective, POP-related analysis, we have declared as survivable.

Brutus REX

Brutus Rex suggests the implementation of living spaces to protect the park from being demolished and thereby to conserve its magic and outlandish romance. Next to the capability of fulfilling individual entitlements of living, *Brutus Rex* is accessible to a multitude of people. The structure plants itself over the park, inserting another, non-destructive, layer of time and space. Four meter high catwalks serve the inhabitants as gateways to the beautiful and mythical parts of the park, the cadavers of POP, without disturbing the ongoing process of "overgrowing."

On POP (architecture)

1// POP needs an audience, obeisance, and, probably, a sort of immolation.

2// Architecture is a service provider. It is a form of expression that defines space and sets the leeway for movements. This means that it also restricts movements. These actions are performed in a society that we presume to be held together by populist thoughts.

3// Amongst others, POP defines itself through its fast pace which is further enhanced by society's throw-away mentality. Since celebrating is a virtue, even the failures of POP elements

The Ferris Wheel in the Spreepark

are applauded, and thereby made publicly available. This can be seen in the behavior of prototype POP stars who are often subject to self-destruction which, however, appears to be deliberately put on stage.

4// Architecture can be – and even has to be – a service provider for products of POP. Architecture may also be the final product of POP, though there is an issue of timing. At the time of its completion it is mostly behind the state-of-the-art. However, by coincidence it may become cutting edge at a later date.

5// POP utilizes the method of sampling. By adding a new theme, material, etc. it may revive and revaluate the past. The product is put out of an existing context into a new one, and thereby it is energized with novel thoughts and feelings.

6// POP acts subversively. The keynote lies within finding a new remix, a preferably extreme expression that has never existed before, or not within the preliminary context.

7// POP is exaggerating – mainly in one specific direction. It is an inflated overstatement. Yet, it works only for a short period of time, and mostly with people who cannot be allocated within POP culture itself.

The translation of these POP aspects has been realized through the definition of a design formula.

POP methods

1// Annihilation: POP is able to neutralize the differences between sub- and high culture. By creating a principle of adaptation that coheres with artistry, and that furthermore is suitable for a mass market, one is able to identify POP as an independent scheme.

2// Transfer: Scientific abilities – that is, analytical methods and technologies of high cultures – are transferred to everyday phenomena. Habitation transcends due to the aestheticization of almost every aspect of living.

3// De- and Re-contextualization: To alienate and prescind an artifact from its habitual context results in a transformation, thereby in a novel appearance of an old entity.

The former restaurant

4// Medium and infrastructure: POP needs the masses, therefore POP needs to be diffused. It stands in correlation with the rise of mass media and bulk articles, which have altered the normal course of life of the majority of the population.

5// Adaptation: Social criticism and subcultures are absorbed and adapted – POP is an accumulative principle.

6// Program of protection: The scheme of POP engages with the mentality of consumption of bulk production without any reservation. On the one hand it promotes the undamped willingness of possessing goods and information – on the other hand it is only partly worthwhile.

Architecture is a service provider.

The *Westerndorf* behind the fences of the former Spreepark – actually around 23 people live here.

Site

Our site encompasses 29.5 hectares, roughly 73 acres, and is located in Berlin-Treptow. It is situated just east of the city center of Berlin, at the borders of the river Spree and north of a forest, the so-called Plänterwald. The transition from the city to the periphery is clearly visible here. The neighboring districts of Friedrichshain and Kreuzberg are characterized by urban inner-city buildings with numerous backyards. Most of these buildings were built in the Wilhelminian Style, a typical architectural style in Berlin in the period of the 19th century (*Gründerzeit*). The area directly adjacent to the Plänterwald is characterized by small allotment gardens (*Schräbergarten*), a series of broad traffic aisles, heterogeneous housing structures, and a vast industrial area. The borough contains vast local recreation expanses, and it borders the neighborhoods around the Oberbaumbrücke, which are known for their vibrant music and youth culture scenes.

The prevailing spacious natural areas around the Spreepark provide a feeling of immersion within the periphery. As there are not many points of reference in that area, people constantly have the feeling of being lost. Further, there are hardly any points of orientation, which may also lead to the fact that only a few Berliners are aware of this location.

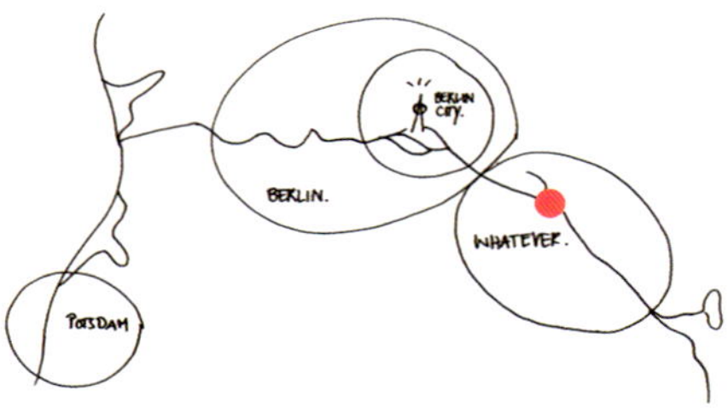

Diagram showing the location of the site

The Allianz towers

The Ferris Wheel of the former Spreepark, seen from the Oberbaumbrücke

The adjacent river Spree is currently solely used by merchant vessels, more or less "touristy" river cruises, and a few private boat owners. The advantages of the waterway are barely utilized, and therefore provide a considerable potential for future development. This area is outstandingly suitable for constructional enhancements based on a POP approach for a series of reasons: It is an area located at the edge of the city boundary, with a distinct historical use, though abandoned and rarely frequented today. Therefore, the site implies geographical, functional, and social components that have the potential to be used for or converted in our POP intervention.

Green spaces

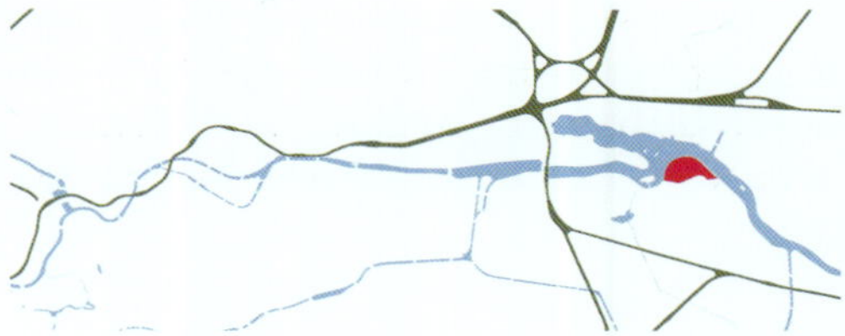

Traffic

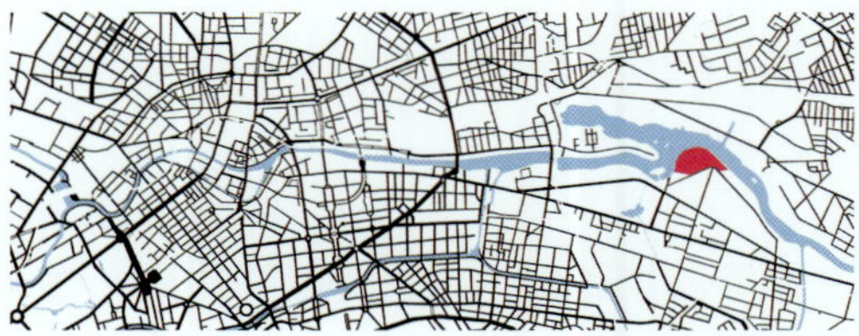

Road network

History

From 1969 to 1989, the amusement park "Cultural Park Plänterwald" was established as the only permanent amusement park in the DDR. In contrast to many Western leisure parks the appearance of this area was rather plain and frugal. A major part of the compound has asphalt covering and permanently installed well-known fun-rides. In addition, the park also consisted of green corridors and functional buildings offering restaurant or lavatory spaces. The greatest attraction of the park was the 45 meter high Ferris Wheel which, already at that time, served as a landmark for the surrounding area. However, today, it has been replaced in its function by the "Treptowers," which are office towers built by the insurance company Allianz in 1998.

After the fall of the Berlin Wall in 1989 the "Cultural Park Plänterwald" was purchased by the West-German investor Norbert Witte, who transformed it into a tiny Berlin-style Disneyland. The name was changed to "Spreepark Berlin," new rides were installed, and it quickly attracted 1.5 million visitors per year – an all-time record. A few years later, the concept of the leisure park was revised and remodeled step-by-step to Western standards. The asphalt covering around the Ferris Wheel was removed and replaced with an aquatic landscape. Furthermore, numerous other rides, such as roller coasters (one containing an enormous loop), two white-water rides, a stage for shows, a Western village, and a traditional English hamlet were installed on the 21 hectares

Plan of the existing fun-rides today

The former Spreepark,
seen from the other side of the river Spree

(52 acres) of used space. Nonetheless, after 1990, the number of visitors sank to 700,000 per year, which was – amongst others – one result of the relatively high admission charges of 30 DM (15 Euros) per person, and due to a lack of parking close to the compound.

Finally, in 2001, the company had to declare their insolvency. Soon afterwards, the owner absconded to Peru in a cloak-and-dagger operation, taking with him all the still-functioning rides, leaving behind his huge debt and abandoning the park. The compound passed into the realty funds of the city of Berlin. Today, the park is completely fenced off, storing the 21 rusting remains of the old fun-rides.

The Spreepark in the '70s

The Spreepark in the '90s

The Saga of Ferris Wheel

When it gets dark it turns cold. Cold and lonely. While being lonely, memories become vivid. Especially on the very top, in the topmost gondola, it seems as if the mist freezes while embracing the wind to first carry thoughts and then withdraw them at once.

Memories appear of a time when the park was still colorful, when voices of people twisted around Ferris Wheel like a carousel or even faster than they would have been at full speed. The Sundays in springtime were especially beautiful. Those days when the sun vitalized the earth and attracted numerous people to occupy the city and its river. When the sound of children's voices accelerate Ferris Wheel a little bit each time they cheer in the gondolas.

But Ferris Wheel has not turned for a long time. It all started with fewer people coming, even on beautiful days. Further, some of its friends have been disposed of, such as Roller Coaster or Catenarian Carousel. Finally, nobody came anymore to ride Ferris Wheel. Sometimes a few people passed by the fence and looked into the park. "Eerie," they said to each other and shook their heads while admiring the mirthless Ferris Wheel that still faced the wind and looked down on its wrecked friends.

On one of those cold and lonely evenings, Ferris Wheel was once again looking sorrowfully towards the city. It could see those newly-erected towers that had taken away its status as a landmark, as well as the glow of yet another buzzing night without sleep. All of a sudden it knew what to do. What the park needed was to once again be a part of the city's life. Slowly the brainchild started to grow. People would need a reason to come back to the park. Maybe it would be best if they stayed there, for good. One has to build a house, a house that provides shelter for all of Ferris Wheel's friends. And when the people would look at the house they should also see Ferris Wheel. So, Ferris Wheel set forth to communicate its plan to the other fun-rides, dreaming that maybe sometime, somebody will ride in the gondolas again to view the silhouette from the topmost point and the city would reflect its visage through the floating river ...

NUR FÜR BESU

Plastic Coated Glade – POP Interventions or Brutus Rex

Analyses / Park elements

As we went to the site, we found it to be very special, with a unique and chaotic character, which, to us, was extremely beautiful. We decided three things: The first thing involved the Ferris Wheel. It is unquestionably the most important part of the world behind the fence, and the only connection with the outside world, the connection to history, the forgotten landmark, the soul of the former Spreepark. It is a sign of joy and better times – still there, but neglected and almost forgotten. We wanted it to come alive again. Secondly, we realized that the process of the overgrowth is a wonderful and strong element of the place, meaning we were not willing to disturb this process. Third, the majority of the existing fun-rides may be defined as crazy POP-Trash. They are beautiful, but dangerous and functionally useless. Somehow, we had to re-organize them and install a new order. Traditional types of architectural analysis seemed to be difficult as the site is surrounded by woods and water, leaving it a forgotten island.

Finally, based on our POP research, we decided to use a very subjective analysis based on our emotions and feelings. First, we analyzed the fun-rides using our own subjective categories. We rated such things as the condition, the mobility, the alternative usage, the "mythological factor," the possibility of inhabitation, and the "romance factor." Based on this analysis we found our "top ten" POP fun-rides. Similar to the process of natural selection, we decided to choose the strongest and most special ones that we wanted to include into the new building. Those ten fun-rides are supposed to support the Ferris Wheel in its quest.

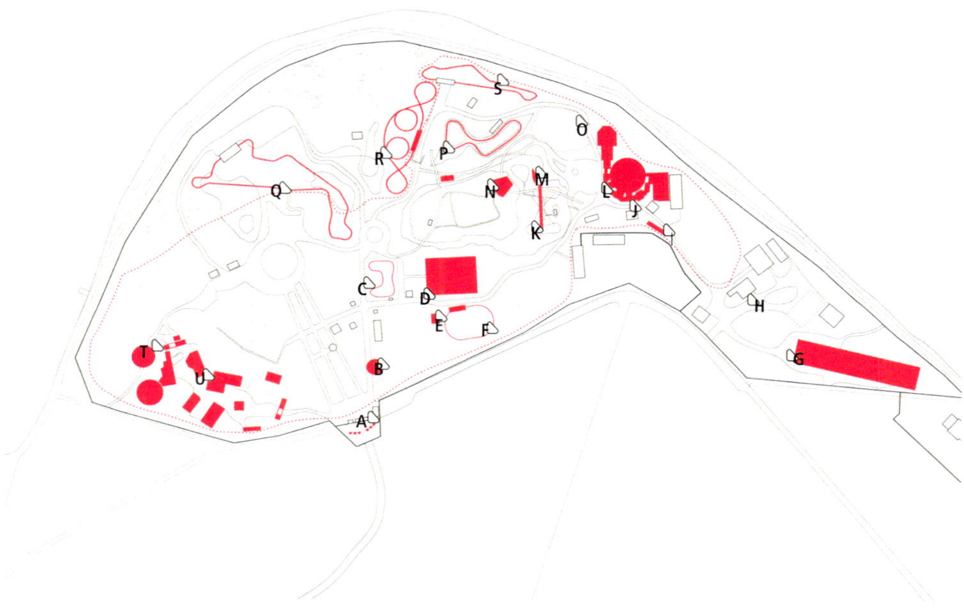

A / Entrance
B / Quick-cup
C / Oldtimer
D / Restaurant

E / Clown-show
F / Kentucky ride
G / Assembly hall
H / Darkride

I / Railway
J / Picadilly tent
K / Big wheel
L / Picadilly cottages

M / Corsair
N / Stands
O / Dino world
P / Swan-ride

Q / Grand canyon
R / Spreeblitz
S / Chaupeau claque
T / Cinema 2000
U / Western village

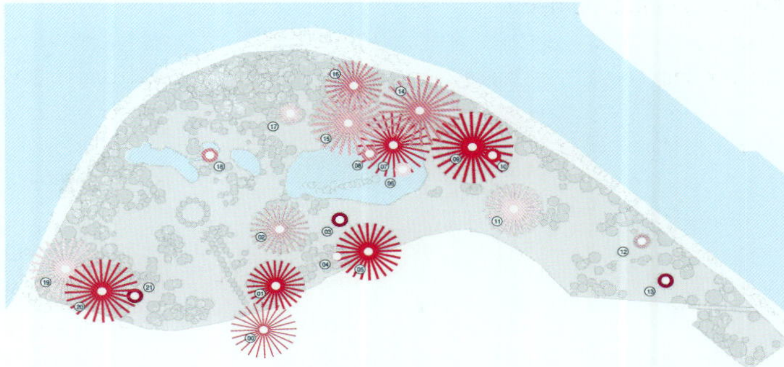

Park analysis
Mobility / condition / alternative usage

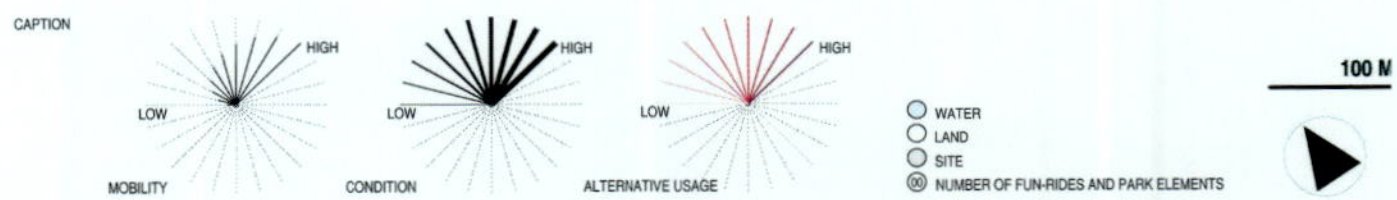

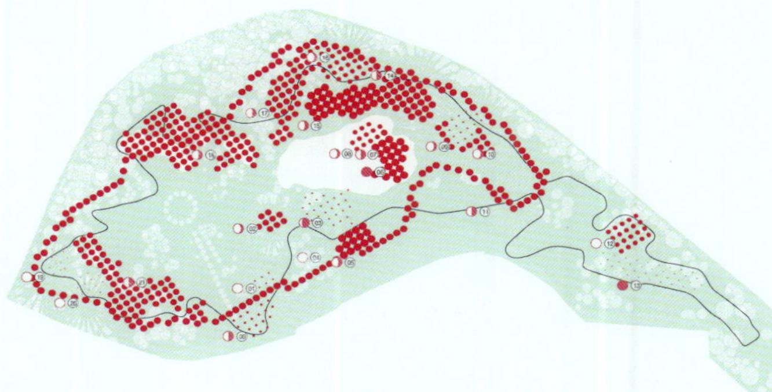

Park analysis
Felt romance / felt myth of the park elements

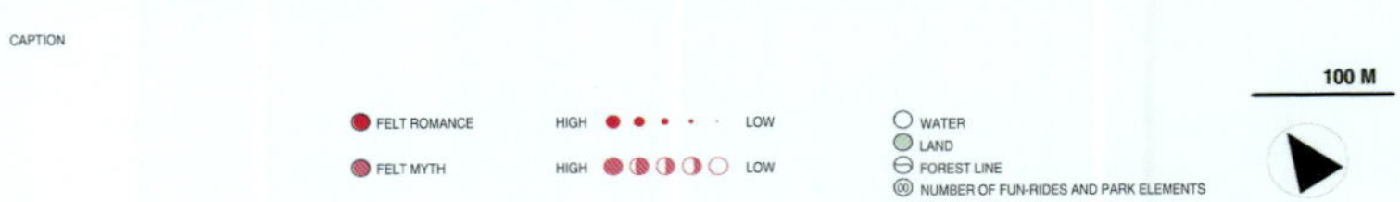

spreeblitz

TARGET GROUP: ALL VISITORS
AREA: CA. 3200 M2

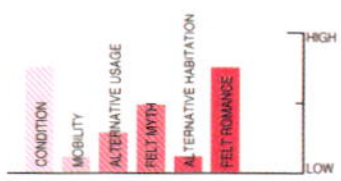

grand canyon

TARGET GROUP: ALL VISITORS
AREA: CA. 5000 M2

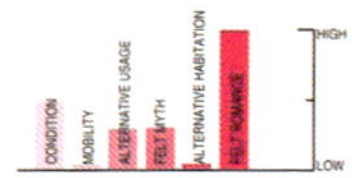

stands

TARGET GROUP: ALL VISITORS
AREA: CA. 600 M2

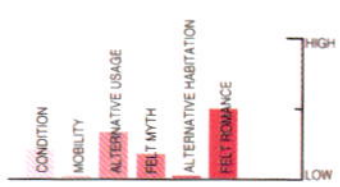

corsair

TARGET GROUP: FAMILIES
AREA: CA. 40 M2

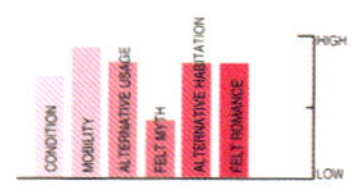

picadilly cottages

TARGET GROUP: ALL VISITORS
AREA: CA. (ALL) 2800 M2

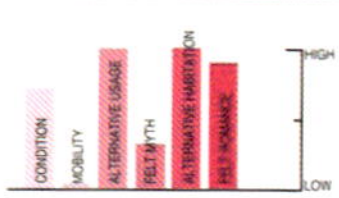

big wheel

TARGET GROUP: ALL VISITORS
AREA: CA. 1320 M2

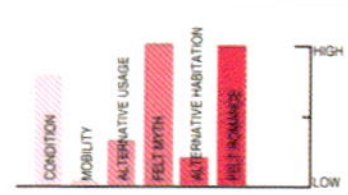

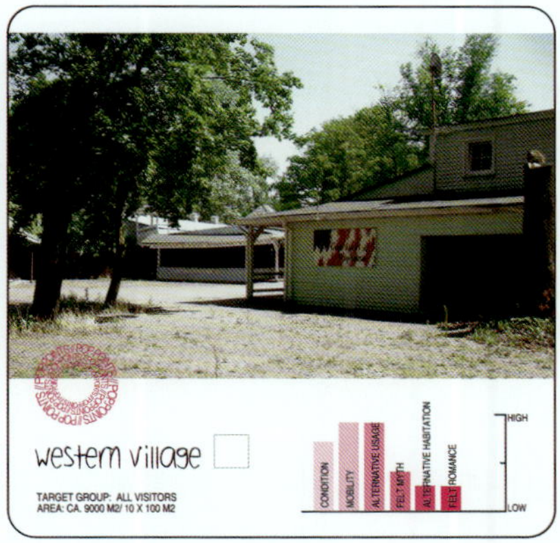

"Top ten" POP fun-rides and the Ferris Wheel
Indication of the condition, mobility, alternative usage, "mythological factor," possibility of inhabitation, and "romance factor."

Method

The soul of the Spreepark is desperately longing for its former popular state of being. The only things which are left today are melancholy, romanticism, and a long-lost pleasure ... As we were interested in an intervention that leaves space for the site's history and its peculiar identity, we wanted to insert new structures which could create a contrast to the existing parts by their outer appearance. We deliberately sought to create a functional patronage of the old via the new. As described above, we rated all the park elements to select those to further work with differing the fun-rides by our self-chosen, subjective categories. Following this analysis, we extracted what we understood to be the "essence" of the fun-rides, eventually decided on a small selection of those rides which we felt to be most important and prominent within the park. Our design suggests a new waterway connected to the river Spree on both ends. In addition, we incorporated and made use of some former park elements, such as the Swan. The grotesque combination of the elements and structures enhances the quality of living in a unique but also humorous way. Nature and the structure embrace each other to create a singular atmosphere for living.

To achieve these goals, we deployed a "mathematical" system, focussing on the Ferris Wheel, which functions as the backbone of the building(s). By expanding it horizontally, we created an object that is able to absorb all the other major fun-rides of the park. They move vertically towards the superstructure to become a part of it, i.e., they are captured by it and thus preserved for posterity.

The Ferris Wheel is clearly noticeable since it is the only object that moves on the horizontal axis. The other rides move perpendicular to it. This method follows our previously defined POP approach. It reevaluates the existing objects by combining them with something new. Furthermore, the structure itself is something novel that can be understood as a conglomerate of samples of the past. Old and new melt together and create an exaggerated statement. The structure is massive, and at the same time it marks the aesthetics of

the overgrown. Together by coincidence. Hence, we decided to structure the object into cubes that serve as entities for living – in the following denoted as "pixels." These pixels are autarkic, thus they can be combined at will.

To allocate the pixels we created the following algorithm:

1// Take the eleven major fun-rides and determine their surface area;

2// Set a standard width for all rides that sum up to the width of the Ferris Wheel;

3// Stretch the surface area to fix the preset width;

4// Calculate the number of pixels by multiplying the romance and myth factor of each ride;

5// Allocate the pixels through a list of percental distribution units.

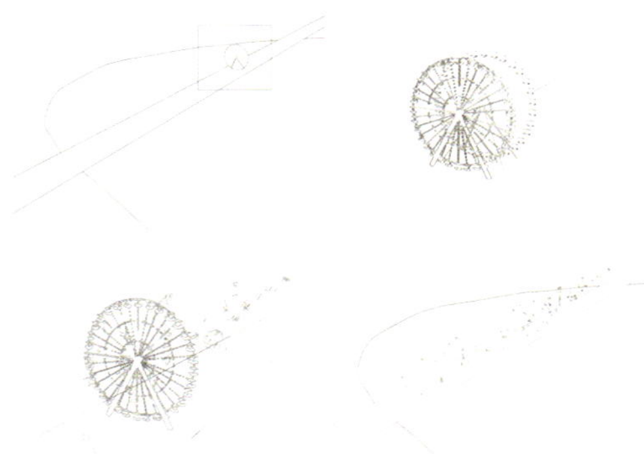

Calculation

The following table summarizes all the factors that are used for allocating the pixels. Each line has to be four meters wide to reach the width of the Ferris Wheel. This width is used to calculate the length based on the surface area. When a ride is too long, such as the roller coaster, we simply cut it to fit in the structure. Furthermore, from our analysis we gathered numerical values from 1 to 10 for the myth and romance factors for the major rides. When multiplying the two factors we get the number of pixels. Since there would not be enough to cover the space we had to quadruple the whole result (i.e., scale up …)

	fun-rides	lenght(m)	romance	myth	pixels (x4)
1	Grand Canyon	432	7	6	168
2	Spreeblitz	450	8	5	160
3	Stands	144	6	2	48
4	Corsair	50	9	2	72
5	Picadilly	340	8	3	96
6	Ferris Wheel	794	10	10	400
7	Railway	2200	9	3	108
8	Restaurant	950	2	4	32
9	Oldtimer	140	8	2	64
10	Western village	910	7	6	168
11	Cinema 2000	360	3	2	24

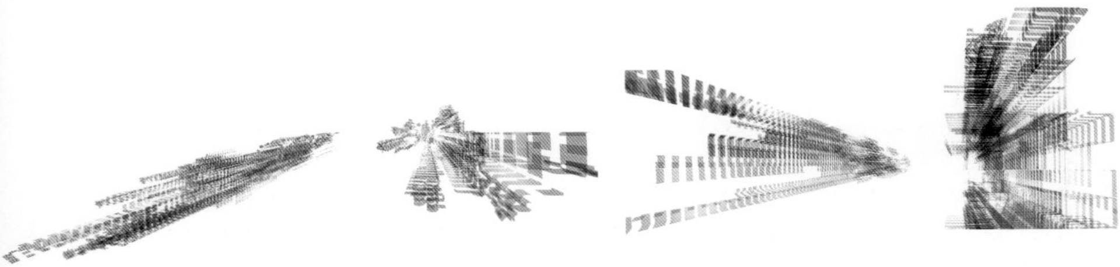

left
Design studies

below
Winter collage

The Ferris Wheel consists of gondolas all placed on a different level of altitude. Since we calculated different volumes of pixels for each ride (i.e., each line), we "stretched" each gondola to the foremost pixel. As a result, the Ferris Wheel spreads through every ride and creates a structure. The next step is to simplify the rather complex structure of the gondolas, as well as the rest of the outline. Due to its circular form, the Ferris Wheel consists of eleven pixels in width and height. We adjusted the stretched overall outline to match this grid. However, to keep the image of the Ferris Wheel, the outlines of the gondolas are still visible on the foremost point of each line of the structure in direction towards the city.

To define the eleven different stripes which were related to the chosen eleven park elements, we sampled the characteristics we found in the park. There are two different concepts. First is the color concept, related to program (POP and mythos or romance), and the other is the nature concept, where we place our "nature" elements within a grid of outdoor and green spaces to support the overgrowing process. Therefore we propose to use steel wire meshes that can themselves be overgrown by nature as time goes by.

The results of our calculations can be summarized as follows:

1// The final structure is 608 meters long, 44 meters high and 44 meters wide;

2// It provides 20.000 square meters of living space;

3// All living units are developed within a 4 by 4 meter steel structure grid;

4// Since the structure operates like (another) superimposed layer, the park can continue to overgrow;

5// The living units are treated as single family houses, all combined in one structure, in order to support the process of the overgrowing, and not to loose the impression of living in a park which is full of public green spaces and private gardens.

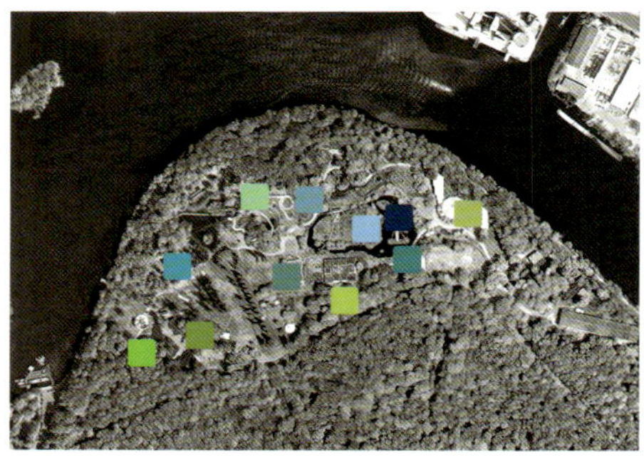

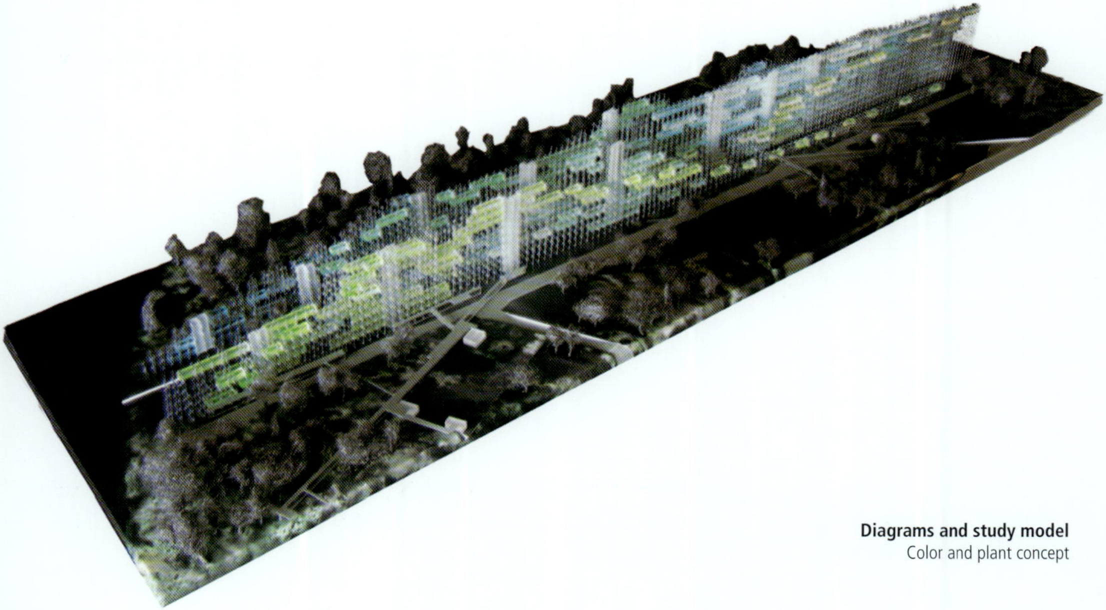

Diagrams and study model
Color and plant concept

/ 32 M ^{2}

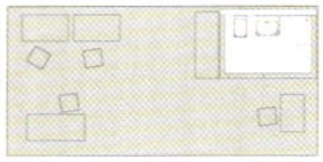

A / OFFICE

/ 32 M ^{2}

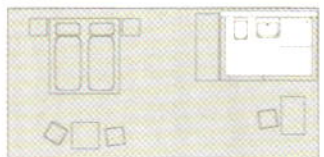

B / SHARED GUEST UNIT

/ 48 M ^{2}

A / LIVING 1

/ 48 M ^{2}

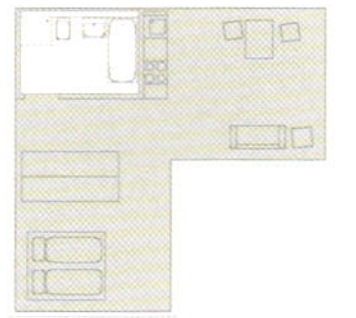

B /LIVING 2

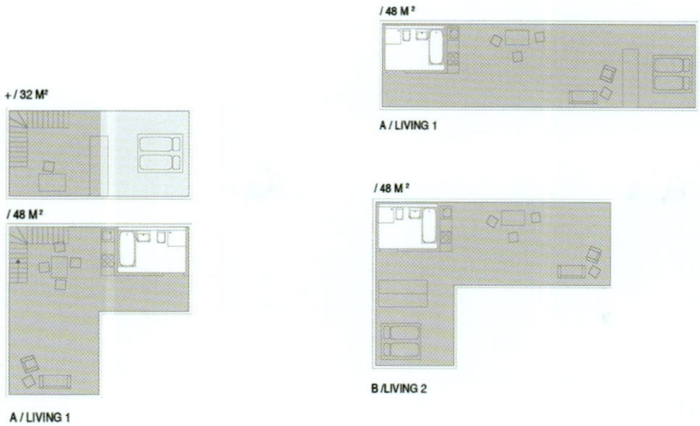

above
Pixel-typologies

below
Inbound views

Functional diagrams

1+2// Metropolitan areas and elevators

The structure is equipped with sixteen staircases and elevators. Their placement is defined through former park elements in combination with the standard guidelines of the German "Fire Protection Guide" (Brandschutzverordnung). With this concept it is possible to provide a high level of privacy in this huge structure. There are even two main entrance points, visible in the diagram below.

3// View points related to the existing fun-rides

The catwalks slide out of the superstructure and can be seen as an additional, four meter high layer floating above the park-level. For pedestrians, the entire circulation through the park area is limited to this level. Therefore, the overgrowing process can continue underneath, while still allowing the residents and visitors to safely observe the most beautiful and romantic points of the park.

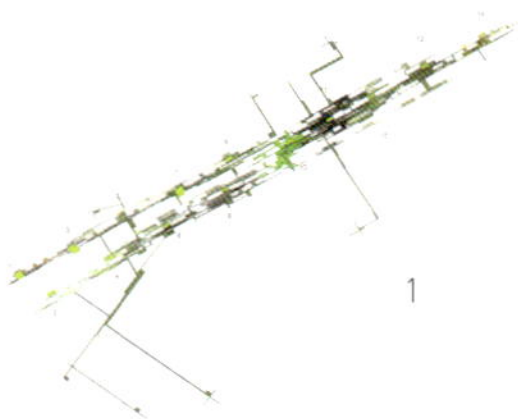

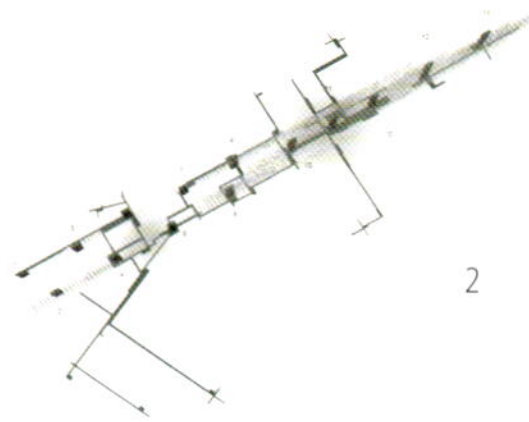

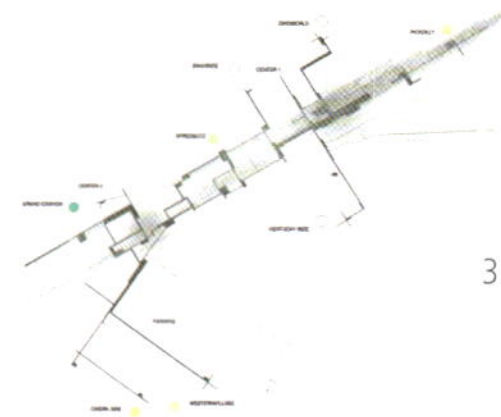

4// Community spaces
There are many community spaces provided in the structure. The majority of them are placed on the upper ground floor level. All of the supporting services for living such as bakeries, laundries, post offices, and kindergardens are placed here, mainly around the entrances. However, there are numerous garden pixels and community spaces scattered all over the structure.

5// Living space
The structure provides more than 20.000 square meters of living space.

6// Parking spaces
Two underground parking spaces provide ca. 400 parking lots, all connected with the main entrance points. We decided to put the pedestrian traffic above the ground level, and opted for putting the car traffic four meters below.

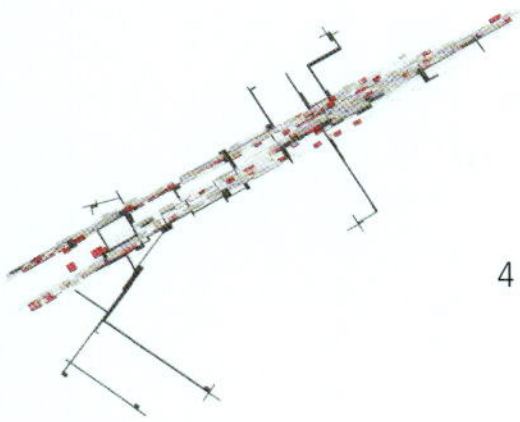

4

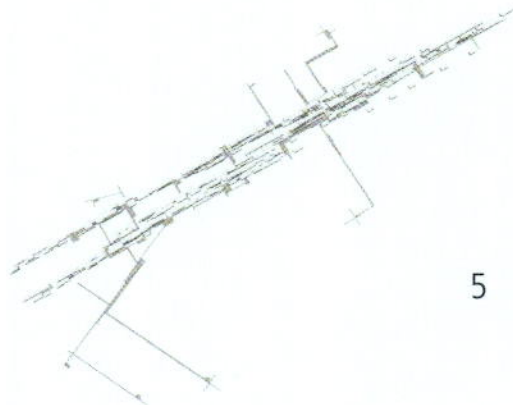

5

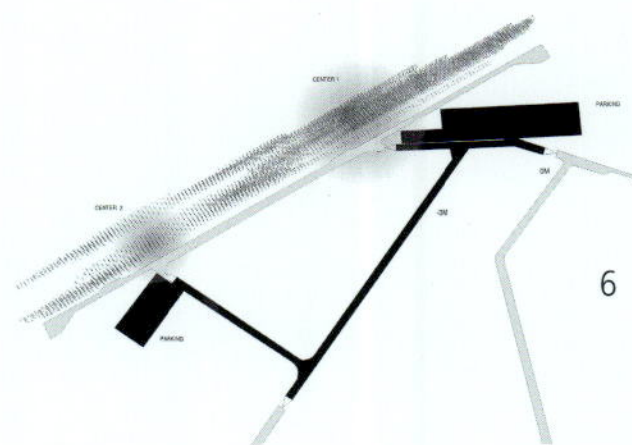

6

Overgrowing and tarnishing

We deliberately decided not to touch or integrate buildings into the park. Neither did we plan to re-nature the area. Instead, *Brutus Rex* suggests the implementation of an enormous superstructure, which covers the glade of the Spreepark and coats it from one end to the other. It should be considered as a "seal" that protects the surface of the park and allows it to continue to grow naturally. But unlike a natural coat, our coat is an artificial one, it is a human-made coat – a *Plastic Coat*. This coating can be understood as an added (most) artificial material marking the natural process of the overgrowth. In regard to POP mechanisms, the *Plastic Coat* is the inverse, but also the counterpart to mainstream operations. Over time, the Spreepark will vanish until nature has recaptured its original space. Living inside this unique environment creates a special atmosphere. It is at the same time orderly, yet agrestal and bloomy, and unfinished. As nature slowly coats the former rides and forms a unity with their inherent joy, gradually, the fun-rides and the Spreepark will form something new, exactly like *Brutus Rex* does. And the inhabitants will be part of this living POP process.

Nature recaptures the park

APPENDIX

EDITORS & AUTHORS

Daniela Konrad, born in 1972, lives and works in Berlin, Germany. In 1999 she graduated in Architecture and Urban Design from the Technische Universität Karlsruhe. She has received a DAAD scholarship and earned a Master of Architecture at the University of Illinois at Chicago in 2000. Since then she has been engaged in a series of teaching and research activities at the University of Illinois at Chicago and at the Bauhaus-Universität Weimar, among others. She has worked for various practices, e.g., Allmann Sattler Wappner Architekten, Skidmore Owings & Merrill LLP (Chicago), and Mattes · Sekiguchi · Partner Architekten. In 2008 she co-founded *Büro KL*. She is currently working as a Wissenschaftliche Mitarbeiterin (Assistant Professor) of architectural design at the Technische Universität Berlin. In 2007 she initiated, together with her colleague Jason Danziger, the experimental symposium "ARCHITECTURE reTURNS to POP."

Jason Danziger, born in 1970, lives and works in Berlin, Germany. He studied sculpture and photography at the University of Massachusetts in Amherst, earning a Bachelor's Degree, Magna Cum Laude, in 1992. He earned a Master of Architecture at the Massachusetts Institute of Technology in 1998. Jason has worked professionally in New York City for Davis Brody Bond and in Athens, Greece for Atelier 66/Suzana & Dimitris Antonakakis, among others. Jason founded *thinkbuild architecture* in 1999. He taught graduate-level design studios at the Technische Universität Berlin as a Wissenschaftlicher Mitarbeiter (Assistant Professor) of architectural design from 2000-2007, and has also taught as a Visiting Professor or Lecturer at a variety of international institutions. Today, he holds a position as a research fellow at ADIP, TU Berlin.

Sandra Bartoli, born in 1967 in the Dolomites, lives and works in Berlin, Germany. She has an education in architecture and landscape architecture. Co-founder of *Terraform* with Andreas Ziegeler in 2000, she is now running with Silvan Linden the *Büro für Konstruktivismus*, which deliberately constructs the universe from its location, right across the Potsdamer Platz. Among their projects are the magazine *Die Planung / A Terv* (as co-publishers and -editors, 2007), the five-storey wall drawing in the *Institute of Vehicle Concepts in the German Aerospace Center (DLR)* in Stuttgart, the installation *Wormholes* in the group exhibition *Domain of the Great Bear* in the Kunstraum München (2006), the workshop for the Master Plan 2010/2100 of the strip mining of Hambach (2007), and the publication *Kristalle* (AdBK Nürnberg Ed., Disko series, 2007). She is currently exploring wormhole-theory in the conversion of a warehouse into the new space of the art gallery "carlier I gebauer" in Berlin.

Valéry Didelon, born in 1972, lives and works in Paris, France. He is a professor, critic and historian in the field of architecture and urban studies. He trained as an architect in France and in the Netherlands in the 1990s, and then studied art history at the Sorbonne, University of Paris. He is now completing his doctoral thesis about the book *Learning from Las Vegas* by Robert Venturi, Denise Scott Brown and Steven Izenour. Since 2001 he has been teaching architecture and theory, and is now at the Ecole Nationale Supérieure d'Architecture de Nantes. He writes for various architecture magazines: *D'architectures, AMC, A+, Faces, Casabella,* etc., and is founder of the new review *Criticat*.

Pedro Gadanho, born in 1968, lives in Lisbon, Portugal and divides his activity between architecture, criticism, curating and teaching. He uses projects, exhibitions or writing to produce critical thinking on the relations between architecture and contemporary culture. He has an MA in Art & Architecture, and a PHD in architecture and mass-media, and currently teaches Theory at the Faculty of Architecture of the Universidade do Porto. He contributes for *A10* and *Blue Design* magazines. Between 2000 and 2003, he was one of the chief curators of *Experimenta Design,* the Lisbon Biennial. Among other exhibitions, he curated *Post-Rotterdam*, for the European Culture Capital Porto 2001, *Space Invaders*, for the British Council, *Metaflux*, the Portuguese representation at the 2004 Architecture Venice Biennale, and, most recently, *Pancho Guedes, An Alternative Modernist,* for the Swiss Architecture Museum, in Basel. His designs include the Ellipse Foundation in Lisbon, and the Orange House in Carreço.

Iassen Markov, born in 1980 in Sofia, Bulgaria, currently lives in Stuttgart, Germany. He studied architecture at the Universität Stuttgart and earned his degree in 2006. From 2006–2007 he worked as a Wissenschaftlicher Mitarbeiter (Assistant Professor) at the chair of Professor Dr. phil. Gerd de Bruyn, *Institut Grundlagen moderner Architektur und Entwerfen* (IGMA) at the Universität Stuttgart, and he has also taught at the Architectural Association in London. Iassen is co-editor of the book *5 Codes: Architektur, Paranoia und Risiko in Zeiten des Terrors.* Today he concentrates on project management in Sofia, Bulgaria, and holds a fellowship from the Akademie Schloss Solitude.

Riklef Rambow, born in 1964, currently lives in Berlin, Germany. In 1992 he graduated in Psychology at the Universität Bielefeld and in 1999 he earned a Dr. phil. nat. from the Universität Frankfurt with a thesis on "Expert-Layperson-Communication in Architecture." Between 1992 and 2001 he taught Educational Psychology at the Universities of Frankfurt/Main and Münster/Westfalen. Since 2001 he has been teaching Architectural Theory and Architectural Psychology at the Brandenburg Technische Universität (BTU) Cottbus, currently with the status of a guest professor. His research is mainly concerned with the perception, communication and everyday use of architecture. He is also a partner in *PSY:PLAN Institute for Architectural and Environmental Psychology*, a consulting practice in Berlin.

Student Authors / Seminar Participants and Diploma Students

The international group of student authors is composed of (listed in alphabetical order): Kalina Aleksandrova (Bulgaria), Andreas Bengtsson (Sweden), Carlos Gor Gomez (Spain), Martin Hartwig (Germany), Julie Hoffmann (Luxemburg), Anna Hyyppä (Finland), Valle Medina Ibáñez (Spain), Will Loft (Australia), Marta Onofre (Portugal), Sybille Paulsen (Germany), Ben Reynolds (Australia), Anna von Roeder (Germany), Karen Rose (Germany), Hege I.R. Schjønhaug (Norway), Berta Sola Sánchez (Spain), and Giulia Tubelli (Italy)

Our diploma students authors are Kai Magnus Bergmann and Uta Böcker (Germany), who by now have successfully earned degrees in Architecture at the TU Berlin, and are currently working as architects in Berlin and in London.

BIBLIOGRAPHY

The bibliography below lists all major text references used in this book, including texts from the World Wide Web. All references from webpages were verified in June, 2008.

0 — INTRODUCTION // POP Phenomena in Architecture

Banham, Reyner. *Apropos the Smithsons.* In: New Statesmen, n°62, September 1961

Banham, Reyner. *A Throw-away Aesthetic.* In: Sparke, Penny (editor). Design By Choice, Academy Editions, London, 1981

Banham, Reyner. *Vehicles of Desire.* In: Leffington, Edward (editor). Modern Dreams: The Rise and Fall and Rise of Pop. The Clocktower Gallery, New York, 1988

Barthes, Roland. *The Eiffel Tower.* In: Leach, Neil (editor). Rethinking Architecture: A Reader in Cultural Theory, Routledge, London and New York, 1997

Barthes, Roland. *Semiology and the Urban.* In: Leach, Neil (editor). Rethinking Architecture: A Reader in Cultural Theory, Routledge, London and New York, 1997

Boehm, Gottfried. *Die Wiederkehr der Bilder.* In: Boehm, Gottfried. Was ist ein Bild? Fink, Müchen, 1994. pg. 30

Bonz, Jochen (editor). *Sound Signatures. Pop-Splitter.* Suhrkamp, Frankfurt/Main, 2001. pg. 10

Bonz, Jochen (editor). *Popkulturtheorie.* Ventil, Mainz, 2002

Boorstin, Daniel. *The Image: A Guide to Pseudo-Events in America.* Vintage, New York, September, 1992

Branzi, Andrea. *No-Stop City: Archizoom Associati.* Editions HYX, Orléans, 2006

Bruyn, Gerd de, Mauler, Henrik and Trüby, Stefan (guest-editors). *Pop, Ökonomie, Aufmerksamkeit.* Archplus, n°171, June 2004

Cohen, Jean-Louis. *Populismus.* In: Archplus, n°162, October 2002

Cook, Peter. *Archigram.* Birkhäuser, Basel, 1991

Eco, Umberto. *Travels in Hyperreality.* Harvest Books, Fort Washington, 1990

Eco, Umberto. *Einführung in die Semiotik.* Fink, München, 2002

Eisenman, Peter. *Duck Soup.* In: LOG 7. Cynthia Davidson (editor). Anyone Corporation, April, 2006

Fiske, John. *Reading the Popular.* Routledge, London, 1989

Foster, Hal. *Image building. (Pop architecture).* In: Artforum International, vol Pop after pop, 2004

Frampton, Kenneth. *Modern Architecture: A Critical History.* Thames & Hudson, London, 4th edition, 2007

Goldberg, Vicki. *Photography in Print: Writings from 1816 to the Present.* University of New Mexico Press, Albuquerque 1981. pg. 521

Hamilton, Richard. *Persuading Image.* In: Leffington, Edward (editor). Modern Dreams: The Rise and Fall and Rise of Pop. The Clocktower Gallery, New York, 1988

Higgins, Dick and Vostell, Wolf. *Poparchitektur. Concept Art*. Droste Verlag, Düsseldorf, 1969

Jencks, Charles. *The iconic building is here to stay.* In: City, vol 10, n°1, April 2006

Koelbl, Herlinde, Sack, Manfred and Mitscherlich, Alexander. *Das deutsche Wohnzimmer.* Bucher, München, 2000

Lefebvre, Henri. *La production de l'espace.* Anthropos, Paris, 1974. pg. 116.

Mitscherlich, Alexander. *Die Unwirtlichkeit unserer Städte: Anstiftung zum Unfrieden.* Suhrkamp, Frankfurt/Main, 25. Auflage, 2006

Pantle, Ulrich. *Partizipation, Alltag, Pop.* In: Bruyn, Gerd de and Trüby, Stefan (editors). Architektur_Theorie.doc. Texte seit 1960. Birkhäuser, Basel, 2003

Rudofsky, Bernard. *Architecture Without Architects. A short introduction to non-pedigreed architecture.* Doubleday & Company, New York, 1964

Scott Brown, Denise. *Lernen vom Pop (1971).* In: Bruyn, Gerd de and Trüby, Stefan (editors). Architektur_Theorie.doc. Texte seit 1960. Birkhäuser, Basel, 2003

Sewing, Werner. *No more learning from Las Vegas.* In: Bruyn, Gerd de and Trüby, Stefan (editors). Architektur_Theorie.doc. Texte seit 1960. Birkhäuser, Basel, 2003

Sklair, Leslie. *Iconic architecture and capitalist globalization.* In: City, vol 10, n°1, April 2006

Smithsons, Alison and Peter. *But Today We Collect Ads.* In: ARK, n°18, November 1957. pg. 48-50

Venturi, Robert and Scott Brown, Denise. *Architecture as Signs and Systems: For a Mannerist Time.* Belknap Press of Harvard University Press, Cambridge, 2004

Venturi, Robert, Scott Brown, Denise and Steven Izenour. *Learning from Las Vegas: The Forgotten Symbolism of Architectural Form.* MIT Press, Cambridge, 1972

Whiteley, Nigel. *Reyner Banham: Historian of the Immediate Future.* MIT Press, Cambridge, 2003

Winter, Rainer and Mikos, Lothar (editors). *Die Fabrikation des Populären: Der John-Fiske-Reader.* Transcript, Bielfeld, 2001

Wolfe, Tom. *From Bauhaus to our House.* Bantam, New York, 1981. pg. 1

1 — THE PERSONAL IS POP // This Was Tomorrow

Bartoli, Sandra, Conrads, Martin, Linden, Silvan, Polyák, Levente and Seviç, Katarina (editors and publishers). *Die Planung / A Terv.* Berlin / Budapest, 2007

Frank, Thomas. *The Conquest of Cool: Business Culture, Counterculture, and the Rise of Hip Consumerism.* The University of Chicago Press, 1427 East 60th Street, Chicago, 1997

Gibson, William. *Idoru.* Putnam Publishing Group, New York, 1996

Gutmair, Ulrich. *William Gibsons "Idoru" betreibt Rasterfahndung in der Zielgruppe.* 1997. In: http://www.art-bag.org/contd/panorama/gutmair.htm

Sammons, Paul M. *Future Noir: The Making of Blade Runner.* HarperCollins Publishers, New York, 1996

Sterling, Bruce. *CATSCAN 5 "Slipstream."* In: http://w2.eff.org/Misc/Publications/Bruce_Sterling/Catscan_columns/catscan.05

Weyand, Björn. *Die totale Hyperrealität. Christian Kracht, Eva Munz und Lukas Nikol besichtigen Kim Jong-Ils Nordkorea, 2006.* In: http://www.sachbuchforschung.de/html/rezensionen_eintrag.php5?id=23

1 — THE PERSONAL IS POP // The Garden of Earthly Delights

Hall, Peter Sir. *To-Morrow: A Peaceful Path to Real Reform.* Routledge, London, 2003

Howard, Ebenezer. *Garden Cities of To-Morrow.* The MIT Press, Cambridge, 1965

Kunstler, J. H.. *The geography of nowhere*. Simon & Schuster, New York, 1993

Lootsma, Bart and Breugem, Inge (editors). *Adriaan Geuze: West 8.* Uitgeverij 010 Publishers, Rotterdam, 1995

Marx, Leo. *The Machine in the Garden: Technology and the Pastoral Ideal in America.* Oxford University Press, New York, 1964

Meikle, Jeffrey L. *Leo Marx's The Machine in the Garden.* Technology and Culture – Volume 44, Number 1, January 2003, pg. 147-159

Richardson, Tim (editor). *Martha Schwartz. Grafische Landschaften.* Birkhäuser, Basel, 2004

Smith, Ken. *Going Through the Scales.* In: http://www.asla.org/land/2006/1017/smith.html

White, Mason. *Notes on the State of American Architecture #2 - Part 2: Faking It For Real.* In: http://www.archinect.com/views/view.php?id=10923_0_36_0_C

Wood, Andrew Dr. *Joel Garreau's Machine and Garden.* In: http://www.sjsu.edu/faculty/wooda/149/149syllabus9marchinegarden.html

2 — PEOPLE'S POP // When Denise Was "Learning from POP"

Cohen, Jean-Louis. *Promesses et impasses du populisme.* Cahiers de la recherche architecturale et urbaine, Janvier 2004

Frampton, Kenneth. *America 1960-1970 notes on urban images and theory.* In: Casabella n°359/360, 1971

Goodman, Robert. *After the Planners.* Simon and Schuster, New York, 1971
Interview with Venturi and Scott Brown. Harvard Architectural Review, I, Spring 1980
Koetter, Fred. *On Robert Venturi, Denise Scott Brown, and Steven Izenour Learning from Las Vegas.* Oppositions, May 1974
Lipstadt, Hélène. *Entretien avec Robert Venturi et Denise Scott Brown.* In: AMC n°39, June 1976
Schulze, Franz. *Chaos as Architecture.* In: Art in America, vol 58, n°4, July-August 1970
Scott Brown, Denise. *Learning from POP.* In: Casabella n°359/360, 1971
Tzonis, Alexander. *In the name of the people.* In: Forum n°3, 1976
Venturi, Robert, Scott Brown, Denise and Steven Izenour. *Learning from Las Vegas: The Forgotten Symbolism of Architectural Form.* MIT Press, Cambridge, 1972

2 — PEOPLE'S POP // Arbeitsamt

Bernays, Edward, Hoffenstein, Samuel, Kingsley, Walter and Pemberton, Murdock. *The Broadway Anthology.* Duffield & Company, New York, 1917
Berne-Joffroy, Andre. *Paul Valéry, ou, La Littérature considérée comme un faux.* Mass Market, Paris, 1987. pg. 35
Blake, William (author) and Bloom, Harold (editor). *The Complete Poetry & Prose of William Blake.* Anchor, London, 1997, pg. 308
Frichot, Hélène. *We owe it to the birds and the trees.* Hélène Frichot speaks to Alain de Botton about "The Architecture of Happiness." In: www.architectureaustralia.com/aa/aaissue.php?issueid=200609&article=9&typeon=1
Gropius, Walter. *Architecture at Harvard University.* Architectural Record, May 1937
Hamlyn, Phillips and Ackroyd, Butler. *William Blake.* Harry N. Abrams, London, 2001, pg. 57
Jones, Jonathan. *Blake's Heaven.* The Guardian, April 25, 2005
Kaufmann, Walter. *Life at the Limits.* McGraw-Hill Education, 1978, pg. 139
Frampton, Kenneth. *The Bauhaus: The evolution of an idea 1919-32.* In: Frampton, Kenneth. *Modern Architecture: A Critical History.* Thames and Hudson, New York, 3rd edition rev., 1992. pg. 124
Lambert, Gilles. *Caravaggio.* Taschen, London, 2005. pg. 8
Lederballe, Lotte Sophie. *Duane Hanson: Sculptures of the American Dream.* Hatje Cantz, Ostfildern, 2007
Maslow, A.H. *A Theory of Human Motivation.* In: Psychological Review, vol 50, 1943. pg. 370-96
O'Hagan, Sean. *Morrissey – So Much to Answer For.* The Observer, Sunday May 6, 2007
Sinderen, Wim van (senior curator, Museum of Photography, The Hague) and Blank, Gil, (FLUENCE Magazine, NYC). *On Exactitudes*. In: http://www.shift.jp.org/en/archives/2005/04/exactitudes.html
Pamer, Laurence (curator, Museum of Art, Fort Lauderdale). *Duane Hanson's Archetypes of Humanity.* In: http://www.broward.org/library/bienes/lii08200.htm

3 — POP(ULARITY) // PEP – POP Education Palace

Carolin, Peter and Fisher, Thomas (editors). Arq: Architectural Research Quarterly: Volume 7, Part 2
Price, Cedric. *The Square Book.* John Wiley & Sons, New York, 2003
Price, Cedric. *Works: v. 2 (Works).* Architectural Association, 1984
Price, Cedric. Obrist, Hans-Ulrich (editor). *Re: CP. With contributions by Arata Isozaki, Patricia Keiller and Rem Koollhaas.* Birkhäuser, Basel, 2003

6 — POP – REINTERPRETED // Plastic Coated Glade – POP Interventions or Brutus Rex

Bonz, Jochen (editor). *Sound Signatures. Pop-Splitter.* Suhrkamp, Frankfurt/Main, 2001
Fiske, John. *Understanding Popular Culture.* Routledge, London, 1989
Gleba, Kerstin and Schumacher, Eckhard. *POP seit 1964.* Kiepenheuer & Witsch, Köln, 2007
Storey, John. *Cultural Theory and Popular Culture: An Introduction.* University of Georgia Press, Athens, 3rd edition, 2001

IMAGE CREDITS

All images in this book are copyrighted to the Technische Universität Berlin, except those listed below. Additionally, the following list names and credits all images that have not been specified in the articles. References from the World Wide Web were verified in June, 2008.

0 — INTRODUCTION

12 Phaeno Center, Wolfsburg, Germany (2007). Architect: Zaha Hadid. Courtesy of Daniela Konrad

14 *Just what is it that makes today's homes so different, so appealing?* Collage, 1956. Artist: Richard Hamilton. Courtesy of Kunsthalle Tübingen, Sammlung G. F. Zundel © VG Bild-Kunst, Bonn 2008

17 "Duck" and "decorated shed" study. Courtesy of Venturi, Scott Brown and Associates

19 Santa Caterina Market, Barcelona, Spain (2005). Architects: EMBT. Courtesy of Daniela Konrad
Mercedes-Benz Museum, Stuttgart, Germany (2007). Architects: UN Studio. Courtesy of Daniela Konrad

20 Eiffel Tower, Paris, France (2006). Courtesy of Daniela Konrad

21 "Eiffel Tower," Hotel *Paris Las Vegas*, Las Vegas, USA. Courtesy of Inga Anger

22 Kunsthaus Graz, Austria. Architects: Peter Cook and Colin Fournier. Courtesy of Antje Veit

24 Row houses, Köln, Germany (2006). Architects: Gruhl Architekten. Courtesy of Daniela Konrad

27 Market place in Krakow, Poland (2007). Courtesy of Daniela Konrad
WideShut. Photo: XTH-berlin © XTH-berlin Janekovic Schröder Rieger Architekten mit Jannes Wurps und Kai Bergmann.

1 — THE PERSONAL IS POP

30 Shanghai, China, 2005. Courtesy of Sandra Bartoli

32 Hydrogen Bomb, mushroom cloud from US nuclear test "Castle Bravo." Bikini Atoll, March 1st, 1954. Photo: U.S. Air Force Airman or employee. As a work of the U.S. federal government, the image or file is in the public domain. Source: http://en.wikipedia.org/wiki/Castle_Bravo
Grandma Vivienne, with Coocoo, Nika and David, Gstaad, 1965. Courtesy of Sandra Bartoli

33 Potsdamer Platz, Berlin, Germany, 2006. Courtesy of Sandra Bartoli

34 *The Pond of Recreation*. Collage: Anna Hyyppä and Hege I.R. Schjønhaug. Courtesy of TU Berlin

44 Advertising image. Collage: Karen Rose and Sybille Paulsen. Courtesy of TU Berlin

2 — PEOPLE'S POP

50/51 Las Vegas Strip, 1970. Courtesy of Venturi, Scott Brown and Associates

52 *Signs of Life: Symbols in the American City.* Exhibition in 1976. Renwick Gallery, Smithsonian Institution, Washington, D.C, USA. Photo: Tom Bernard. Courtesy of Venturi, Scott Brown and Associates

54 Approach. Rendering: Ben Reynolds. Courtesy of TU Berlin

58/59 Battersea, London, 2006. Photos: JoAnn Kneedler © JoAnn Kneedler

60 *Exactitudes 82. French Touch – Bordeaux 2006*. Artists: Ari Versluis and Ellie Uyttenbroek © Ari Versluis and Ellie Uyttenbroek

68 Shopping inside a "biological plant cell." Collage: Kalina Aleksandrova and Julie Hoffmann. Courtesy of TU Berlin

3 — POP(ULARITY)

74 Riklef Rambow's sketchbook. Courtesy of Riklef Rambow

77 In Barceloneta, Barcelona, Spain (2005). Courtesy of Daniela Konrad

78 A madeleine. Courtesy of Jason Danziger

4 — THE ECONOMICS OF POP

5 — VISUAL POP

6 — POP – REINTERPRETED

ACKNOWLEDGEMENTS

We would like to thank everybody who morally, editorially, financially, intellectually, and technically supported the realization of this project. Without all these contributions this publication would not have been possible.

Specifically, we thank the Technische Universität Berlin for supporting the larger project. Our sincere thanks go to ADIP – Fachgebiet für Entwerfen und Innenraumplanung (chair for Architectural Design and Interior Design) – and to Guest Professor Francis Soler, for supporting our vision and enabling us to explore this topic and method with great freedom. Furthermore we want to thank the whole ADIP team for their help and understanding, and especially Bärbel Rost for her everlasting support on all administrative issues.

A special thanks goes to Jennifer Mack for her sublime input and support.

A well-deserved thanks goes to the whole publication team. To Christoph Bukowski for his engaging work on the layout and his excellent input on all graphical and print-related topics. To Samsarah Lilja for her fabulous contribution with initial editing of all incoming texts, and the many good discussions on POP architecture. To Sybille Paulsen for her great contributions to the preparation and the realization of the layout, which amazingly continued even while she was on exchange in the city of Copenhagen, Denmark. To Lisa Plücker for her outstanding layout-work, for her inspirations while putting the final touches to our book, as well as for the design of the cover page.

Furthermore, we would like to thank everybody who took part in this endeavor: our symposium participants, guest critics, special guests and, last but not least, the design seminar participants.

Symposium Participants. Sandra Bartoli, Valéry Didelon, Pedro Gadanho, Iassen Markov, and Riklef Rambow.

Guest Critics. Kai Magnus Bergmann, Uta Böcker, Nancy Couling, Birgit Klauck, Jana Richter, Ali Saad, Joachim Schultz, and Vesta Nele Zareh.

Special Guests. We would also like to thank the following members of the Bauhaus Kolleg VIII – EU Urbanism (2006/7), who provided excellent and substantial constructive criticism to our students during the project: Ursula Achternkamp, Anna Baltschun, Maria Azevedo Coutinho, Bianca Custodio, Marthe Gendron, Onur Kemal Kösedag, Alexandre Mussche, Ursula Daniel Smith, and Banu Tomruk.

Design Seminar Participants. Claudia Afonso, Kalina Aleksandrova, Andreas Bengtsson, Anna Busiakiewicz, Carlos Gor Gomez, Martin Hartwig, Martha Hitner Dos Santos, Julie Hoffmann, Anna Hyyppä, Zornitsa Kirilova, Charlotte Korfmacher, Verena Kühne, Yvonne Lewanscheck, Emilio Liébanas Hidalgo, Samsarah Lilja, Will Loft, Ivana Maras, Valle Medina Ibáñez, Ingo Nolte, Marta Onofre, Jongki Park, Sybille Paulsen, Antonio Perez Blanco, Anne Prellwitz, Jose Ramos, Ben Reynolds, Anna von Roeder, Karen Rose, Gabriela Salazar, Hege I.R. Schjønhaug, Katrin Schwarz, Doreen Smolensky, Berta Sola Sánchez, Daniel Strassburger, Susan Studnitschka, Giulia Tubelli, Franz von Wietersheim, and Anne-Christin Wolf.

This publication has been made possible thanks to a generous donation by Stephan and Barbara Konrad. In addition, the following firms have financially supported this publication (listed in alphabetical order): FSB, Gravis, InformationsZentrum Beton, and Zumtobel. We also thank the firms Eternit, Rheinzink, and Zumtobel for their financial contribution to our symposium "ARCHIETCURE reTURNS to POP" at the TU Berlin in March 2007.

Apple Computer,
iPod und mehr ...